BAB

With the birth of a baby, the search for a beautiful name begins. Relatives and friends are pressed into service, the great Indian epics are often gone through, and the hundred and one names of gods and goddesses are rehearsed, to find a suitable name which will adequately reflect a particular virtue, an aesthetic value, or a religious affinity. To help you with the search, here are nearly 4000 Indian names from the scores of the texts the authoress went through. A handy book in need, the alphabetical arrangement will help you find a name, short or long, to balance with the surname or maintain a tradition.

An appropriate name is important; the child will have to carry it forever. The book therefore gives you an ample choice.

Mrs Vimla Patil is currently the Editor of *Femina*. Rupa has already published her basic cookbook *Dal Roti*.

DAL ROTI

Dal and Roti are the main sources of nutrition for a vast number of Indians, and each region embellishes these dishes by adding fish, meat, coconut milk, cream, vegetables, nuts, and a host of aromatic spices. This book features distinctive preparations from all over India, and describes their making in easy-to-follow steps.

This is not a fancy, coffee table book of cookery: it is down to earth in its approach and content, focusing attention as it does on the basic constituents of an Indian meal.

Baby Names

―――― OVER 4000 ――――
BEAUTIFUL INDIAN NAMES FOR YOUR CHILD

VIMLA PATIL

Rupa & Co

© Vimla Patil 1988

An Original Rupa Paperback
First published 1988
Twenty-first impression 1999

Published by
Rupa & Co
15 Bankim Chatterjee Street, Calcutta 700 073
135 South Malaka, Allahabad 211 001
P. G. Solanki Path, Lamington Road, Bombay 400 007
7/16, Ansari Road, Daryaganj, New Delhi 110 002

Cover designed by J.M.S. Rawat

Typeset by
New Statesman Press
13 Rani Jhansi Road
New Delhi 110 055

Printed in India by
Ahad Enterprises
2609 Baradari, Ballimaran
Delhi 110 006

Rs 40

INTRODUCTION

No one really knows how the practice of naming men and women—and even animals and birds—came about. The most rational explanation seems to be that after the discovery of fire, the nomadic human race started colonizing the best and safest parts of the forest and there arose the need for identifying each member of the community by a symbolic name. It is possible that the first names that occurred to these nomadic races were names of animals, trees and forest spirits, river deities and the many pagan gods and goddesses they worshipped.

But time passed and man became more and more conscious of his intellect and emotions and began to find, in addition to the need, a reason for naming a person. His sensitivity, pride, confidence and sense of belonging grew and he experienced the finer emotions of compassion, fairness, love and affection and these in turn changed his way of looking at the world and other human beings. No longer was survival his sole concern. Since he grew his foodgrains and fruits, he had time to gaze in wonder at Nature's beauty, to name each fragrant flower, each splendid plumed bird, each cascading river and each phenomenon of nature. His deities also became more beautiful and acquired in his mind shapes of beauty and delicacy. Man learnt gradually to be a seeker and worshipper of beauty.

This growing sensitivity was perhaps reflected in the names he gave to his wives and children. Girls were named after birds, flowers, deities or the softer qualities of a woman, and boys were named after the gods and the qualities of valour, honour, bravery, joy

As the family system developed it became a custom for each family to have a separate surname derived either from the village or tribe they belonged to or from the kind of work they did for a livelihood.

The system of names and surnames became highly complex over a period of centuries because of the caste system, because of the innumerable invasions of India and because of faster communications in the last few decades. Inhibitions crumbled with education and the more progressive among people began to name their offspring with care and selectivity. Perhaps this is how pet names or short names originated.

Even today, in Indian society, the orthodox can recognize the caste, community, work or place of origin by the surname of a person Even today names are derived from flowers, birds, nature and mythical deities of all kinds. In more aristocratic families, as elsewhere, so in India too, there is a continuity of names and boys and girls are named after their illustrious ancestors. The ordinary people choose names depending on their education, awareness, sensitivity, family tradition and sometimes even a whim or fancy.

It is common practice to give a child more than one name. Usually the main name is chosen by casting the horoscope and working out the conjunction of favourable planets. Other names are given by the elders or friends of the family. Once named, a boy continues with his name for a lifetime. In the case of a woman, her bridegroom can change her name to one that he likes during the marriage ceremony.

The Hindu sacrament of naming a child is variously called *Naamkaran, Barsa, Peyarsootal, Hasaru edo habba*.

The ceremony is usually held within twelve days of birth. The cradle is decorated with flowers and sweets made from milk; nuts and sugar are distributed to all. A boy is welcomed with more elaborate feasting in the predominantly male dominated society of India.

Both the baby and the new mother receive gifts of cloth, silverware, baby clothes, linen and toys. The eldest woman in the family whispers the chosen name in the ears of the child. In urban areas the child's birth and name are registered with the city council. Apart from the given names, a child often has pet names and names given according to his or her position in the family; e.g., an elder brother is called Dada or Bhaisaab or Anna according to family tradition.

Today, with ethnic names becoming more popular than ever, people turn to the old sources for finding attractive names. These sources are the Vedic texts, the Upanishads, the *Ramayana*, the *Mahabharata* and other ancient literary works. I have myself researched Sanskrit dictionaries, the *Durga Saptashati*, the *Ganesh Kavacham*, the *Vishnu Sahasranama*, the *Ramayana* and the *Mahabharata* to make this collection. Although each name may have several meanings, only the most important and common ones are given in the collection.

Parents who remain ever vigilant to find unusual and pretty names for their children will find that this book puts together a vast number of names as a guideline. I shall feel happy if this book helps parents choose names from it directly or assists them in creating new names.

Vimla Patil

This book is for my husband
PRABHAKAR
and children
NAISHADH and MONISHA
who are as beautiful as their names

Author's Note

Most of the names contained in this book are from the original Sanskrit. I am aware that each name has several variations. For instance, Chandra (m), the moon, can become Chandrabhan, Chandraketu, Chandrakant, Chandramohan, Srichandra, Chandrakiran.

In the case of a woman, Chandra (f), the moon, can become Chandrakala, Chandrabala, Chandralekha, etc.

Thus many standard and local suffixes and prefixes can create innumerable variations from one name. Common prefixes are Shri, Su and others, while common suffixes are Kumar, Dev, Ranjan, Chandra, etc.

Secondly, many names have local variations. For example, Vimla (f), becomes Bimala in Bengal, Vimala in South India, and Vimal in Maharashtra.

Ravindra (m), becomes Rabindra in Bengal, Ravindran in South India, and Ravinder in the Punjab.

Rajendra (m), becomes Rajinder in the Punjab and Rajendran in South India.

Therefore, variations and regional forms being too numerous for inclusion in this book, I have adhered to the original Sanskritized names only. Common forms of all names are included, e.g. although Savitra (m), the sun is truly of neuter gender we have accepted its common feminine form 'Savita'. Local spellings and variations have been left to the users. Also, no such list can be complete or comprehensive. Users of this book may send new names (not included in this edition) to me care of the publisher of this book, and I shall try to include them in the next edition to make it more comprehensive and useful.

V.P.

A

Aadi (m), first; most important

Aafreen (m & f), encouragement

Aakar (m), shape

Aalap (m), musical prelude, conversation

Aandaleeb (m), the bulbul bird

Abbas (m), a family name

Abha (f), lustrous beauty

Abhay (m), fearless

Abheek (m), fearless

Abhijit (m), victorious

Abhilash (m), desire

Abhimanyu (m), Arjuna's son

Abhinav (m), novel

Abhirup (m), pleasing

Abhishek (m), an auspicious bath for a deity; anointing

Abhra (m), cloud

Aboli (f), the name of a flower

Achal (m), constant

Achala (f), constant

Achintya (m), inconceivable; a name of Lord Shiva

Achyut (m), imperishable; a name of Vishnu

Adarsh (m & f), ideal

Adesh (m), command

Adhik (m), greater

Adhira (f), lightning

Adil (m), sincere; just

Adinath (m), the first lord (Lord Vishnu)

Adishree (f), exalted dignity

Adit (m), from the beginning

Aditi (f), the earth

Aditya (m), the sun

Adrika (f), celestial maiden

Adwaita (m), non-duality

Adway (m), one; united

Aftab, Aftaab (m), the sun

Agasti, Agastya (m), name of a sage

Agha (m), pre-eminent

Aghat (m), destroyer of sin

Agharna (m), the moon

Agniprava (m), bright as the fire

Agrata (f), leadership

Agrim (m), leader; first

Agrima (f), leadership

Agriya (m), first; best

Ahalya (f), wife of Rishi Gautam, a woman who was saved by Lord Rama

Ahsan (m), mercy

Aijaz (m), favour

Aiman (m), fearless
Ainesh (m), the sun's glory
Aishani (f), Goddess Durga
Aishwarya (f), wealth
Ajanta (f), a famous Buddhist cave
Ajay (m), invincible
Ajit (m), invincible
Ajitesh (m), Vishnu
Ajmal (m), pious
Ajamil (m), a mythological king
Akalmash (m), stainless; untainted
Akash (m), the sky
Akbar (m), powerful
Akhil (m), complete
Akhila (f), total
Akhilesh (m), lord of all
Akmal (m), complete
Akram (m), excellent
Akroor (m), kind
Akshan (m), eye
Akshar (m), imperishable
Akshath (m), indestructible
Akshay (m), indestructible
Akshaya (f), indestructible
Akshit (m), permanent
Akshita (f), seen
Akul (m), a name of Lord Shiva
Alaknanda (f), a river in the Himalayas
Alam, Aalam (m), the whole world
Alamgir (m), the lord of the whole world
Aleem (m), knowledgeable
Alhad (m), joy
Ali (m), protected by god
Alisha (f), protected by god
Alaka, Alka (f), a girl with a lovely hair
Almas (f), a diamond
Alok (m), a man with lovely hair
Aloke (m), light
Alpana (f), a decorative design
Amal (m), unblemished; pure
Amala, Amla (f), the pure one
Amalendu (m), the unblemished moon
Amalesh (m), the pure one
Amartya (m), immortal
Amber (m), the sky
Ambarish (m), the sky
Ambika (f), Goddess Parvati
Ambuj (m), lotus
Ambuja (f), born of a Lotus; Goddess Lakshmi
Ameya (m), immeasurable
Amil (m), invaluable
Amin, Ameen (m), divine grace
Amir (m), rich
Amit (m), without limit

Amitbikram (m), limitless prowess
Amitjyoti (m), limitless brightness
Amita (f), without limit
Amitabha, Amitav (m), limitless lustre; name of Lord Buddha
Amitrasudan (m), destroyer of enemies
Amiya (m), nectar; delight
Amlan (m), unfading; everbright
Amlankusum (m), unfading flower
Ammar (m), the maker
Amod (m), pleasure
Amodini (f), joyful
Amogh (m), a name of Lord Ganesh
Amol (m), priceless
Amolik, Amolak (m), priceless
Amrapali (f), famous courtesan who became a devotee of Buddha
Amrit, Amrik (m), nectar
Amrita (f), immortality
Amritkala (f), nectarine art
Amrusha (f), sudden
Amulya (m), priceless
Anadi (m), eternal
Anagha (f), sinless
Anahita (f), graceful
Anal (m), fire

Anala (f), fiery
Anamika (f), ring-finger
Anamitra (m), the sun
Ananda, Anand (m), joy; happiness
Anandamayi (f), full of joy
Anandi (f), jovial
Anandini (f), joyful
Ananga, Anang (m), name of Cupid or Kamadeva
Ananya (f), without a second
Ananta, Anant (m), infinite
Anarghya (m), priceless
Anchal (f), the decorative end of a sari
Angad (m), an ornament
Angana (f), an auspicious or handsome woman
Angarika (f), a flame-coloured flower (Palash or Flame of the Forest)
Anil (m), the wind god
Animish, Animesh (m), open-eyed (therefore attractive)
Anirudhha (m), free; grandson of Lord Krishna
Anirvan (m), undying
Anish (m), Lord Vishnu; Lord Shiva
Anisha (f), uninterrupted
Anita* (f), grace

---

*A very common name in India, although it is English.

Anjali (f), offering with both hands

Anjana (f), mother of Hanuman

Anjum (m), a token

Anjuman (m), a token; a symbol

Anju (f), one who lives in the heart

Anjushri, Anjushree (f), dear to one's heart

Ankur (m), sprout, new life

Ankush (m), check; an instrument used for guiding elephants

Anindita (f), beautiful

Anmol (m), priceless

Annapurna (f), Goddess Parvati; generous with food

Anshu (m), the sun

Anshula (f), sunny

Anshuman (m), the sun

Anshumat (m), luminous

Anasuya, Anasooya (f), wife of Rishi Atri

Antara (f), the second note in Hindustani classical music

Anu (m), an atom

Anuj (m), younger brother

Anuja (f), younger sister

Anumati (f), consent

Anunay (m), supplication; consolation

Anup, Anoop (m), without comparison

Anupam (m), without comparison

Anupama (f), without equal

Anuradha (f), name of a star

Anurag, Anuraag (m), love

Anuttam (m), unsurpassed

Anuva (f), knowledge

Anwar (m), devotee of God

Anwesha (f), quest

Apala (f), name of a learned woman of the past

Aparajito (m), undefeated

Aparajita (f), undefeated; name of a flower

Aparna (f), Goddess Parvati

Apsara (f), celestial maiden

Apurva, Apoorva (f), unique

Apurva, Apoorva (m), unique

Aradhana (f), worship

Arati, Aaarti (f), worship with lamps

Arav (m) peaceful

Archa (f), worship

Archan (m), worship

Archana (f), worship

Archit (m), worshipped

Ardhendu (m), half moon

Arghya (m), offering (to the Lord)

Arhant (m), destroyer of enemies
Arindam (m), destroyer of enemies
Arjit (m), earned
Arjun (m), Pandava prince; bright
Arka (m), the sun
Arnav (m), ocean
Arnesh (m), lord of the sea
Arpana (f), surrendered
Arpita (f), dedicated
Arshad (m), pious
Arshia (f), heavenly
Arun, Aroon (m), mythical charioteer of the sun; dawn
Arundhati (f), a star
Aruni (m), name of a devoted pupil
Arunima (f), glow of dawn
Arvind (m), lotus
Arvinda, Arabinda (m), lotus
Aryaman (m), the sun
Asao, Asav (m), essence
Asavari (f), name of a raga or melody
Aseem, Ashim (m), limitless
Aseema, Ashima (f), limitless
Asgar (m), devotee
Asgari (f), devotee
Asha (f), hope, aspiration
Ashis (m), benediction
Ashna (f), friend
Ashok (m), without grief
Ashoka (f), without grief
Ashraf (m), without grief
Ashu (m), quick
Ashutosh (m), Lord Shiva
Ashwin, Asvin (m), a Hindu month
Ashwini (m & f), a star
Asim, Aseem (m), limitless
Asit, Ashit (m), the planet Saturn; dark
Asita (f), the river Yamuna
Aslam (m), greeting
Aslesh (m), embrace
Aslesha (f), a star
Asmita (f), pride
Atanu (m), Cupid
Atal (m), immoveable
Atasi (f), a blue flower
Atma (m), soul
Atmaja (m), son
Atmaja (f), daughter
Atmananda (m), bliss of soul
Atreyi (f), name of a river
Atul, Atulya (m), matchless
Avadhesh (m), King Dasaratha
Avani, Abani (f), earth
Avanindra (m), lord of the earth
Avanish (m), lord of the earth
Avanti (f), ancient Malwa; Ujjain

Avantika (f), city of Ujjain
Avinash (m), indestructible
Avkash (m), limitless space
Avatar (m), incarnation
Ayesha (f), daughter of the Prophet

Azeez (m), friend
Azhar (m), famous
Aziza (f), a friend
Azzam (m), the lord; Almighty

B

Badal (m), cloud; rain
Badri (m), Lord Vishnu
Badrinath (m), Lord Vishnu
Bahubali (m), a Jain Tirthankar
Bahula (f), a star
Bahuleya (m), Lord Kartikeya
Baidehi (f), Sita
Baijayanti (f), garland of Lord Vishnu
Baisakhi (f), of the month Baishakh
Baishali (f), an ancient city
Bajrang (m), a name of Lord Hanuman
Bakul (f), the name of a flower
Bala (f), girl
Balbir (m), strong
Baldev (m), strong
Balgopal (m), baby Krishna
Balagovind (m), baby Krishna
Balakrishna (m), baby Krishna
Balaraj (m), strong
Balaram (m), the brother of Lord Krishna
Ballari (f), creeper
Balvindra, Balvinder (m), strong
Balwant (m), strong
Banamala (f), forests
Banani (f), forests
Banbihari (m), Lord Krishna
Bandana (f), worship
Bandhu (m), friend
Bandhul (m), pleasing
Banhi (f), fire
Banhishikha (f), flame
Banita (f), woman
Bankebihari (m), Lord Krishna
Bankim (m), curved
Bankimchandra (m), crescent moon
Bansari (f), flute
Bansi (m), flute
Bansilal (m), Lord Krishna
Bansuri (f), flute
Barid (m), cloud
Baridbaran (m), colour of the cloud
Barindra (m), the ocean
Barsha (f), rain
Barun (m), Lord of the Sea
Baruna (f), wife of the Lord of the Sea
Baruni (f), Goddess Durga
Basabi (f), wife of Lord Indra
Basanta (m), spring
Basanti (f), of spring

Bashir (m), harbinger of good tidings

Basistha (m), a sage

Basudha (m), earth

Bela, Beli (f), a flower (jasmine)

Benazir (f), incomparable

Bhadra (f), gentle

Bhagirath (m), the king who brought the celestial Ganga to the earth

Bhagirathi (f), the river Ganga

Bhajan (m), adoration

Bhagwant (m), fortunate

Bhagwanti (f), lucky

Bhagya (f), luck

Bhagyaraj (m), lord of luck

Bhagyawati (f), fortunate

Bhairav (m), Lord Shiva

Bhairavi (f), Goddess Durga

Bhakti (f), devotion

Bhamini (f), woman

Bhanu (m), the sun

Bhanudas (m), a devotee of the sun

Bhanumati (f), full of lustre

Bhanupriya (f), beloved of the sun

Bharadwaj (m), a sage; a mythical bird

Bharat (m), son of Shakuntala and founder of Bharat or India

Bharati (f), Goddess Saraswati

Bhargava (m), Lord Shiva

Bhargavi (f), Goddess Durga

Bhaskar (m), the sun

Bhavini (f), Goddess Parvati

Bhaumik (m), attached to the earth

Bhavana, Bhavna (f), meditation; thinking

Bhilangana (f), a river

Bhishma (m), one who has taken a terrible vow

Bhoomi (f), the earth

Bhoomika (f), the earth

Bhooshan (m), decoration

Bhooshit (m), decorated

Bhuvanesh (m), the lord of the world (Vishnu)

Bibek (m), conscience

Bibhas (m), a raga

Bibhavasu (m), the sun; fire

Bikram (m), prowess

Bilva (m), a sacred leaf

Bimal (m), pure

Bimala (f), pure

Binata (f), the wife of Sage Kashyap

Bindu (f), a drop

Binodini (f), handsome; beautiful Radha

Bipasha (f), a river; Beas

Bishakha (f), a star

Bitasok (m), one who does not mourn
Bodhan (m), kindling
Bodhisattva (m), Lord Buddha
Boudhayan (m), the name of a sage
Brahmabrata (m), ascetic
Brahmadutt (m), dedicated to Lord Brahma
Bratati (f), creeper
Bratindra (m), devoted to right deeds
Brijmohan (m), Lord Krishna
Brinda (f), the basil plant; Radha
Buddhadeva (m), Gautama Buddha
Budhil (m), learned
Bulbul (f), a songbird
Bulbuli (f), a songbird

See also entries under *V*

C

Chahna (f), love
Chaitan (f), consciousness
Chaitali (f), born in the month of Chaitra
Chaitanya (m), the name of a saint; consciousness
Chakor (m), a bird enamoured of the moon
Chakori (f), a bird enamoured of the moon
Chakradhar (m), Lord Vishnu
Chakrapani (m), Lord Vishnu
Chakshu (m), eye
Chaman (m), garden
Chamanlal (m), garden
Chameli (f), jasmine
Champa (f), a flower
Champabati (f), the capital of Karna
Champak (m), a flower
Champakali (f), a bud of champa
Chanchal (m), restless; quick
Chanchala (f), restless; quick
Chandak (m), the moon
Chandan (m), sandalwood
Chandana (f), parrot
Chandani (f), a river
Chandanika (f), diminutive of Chandana
Chandika (f), Goddess Parvati
Chandni (f), moonlit
Chandrabali (f), Krishna's girl-friend
Chandrabhaga (f), river Chenab
Chandrabhan (m), the moon
Chandrabhushan (m), Lord Shiva
Chandrachur (m), Lord Shiva
Chandrakala (f), moonbeams
Chandrakanta (m), the moon
Chandrakin (f), a peacock
Chandrakishore (m), the moon
Chandrakumar (m), the moon
Chandralekha (f), a ray of the moon
Chandramohan (m), attractive like the moon
Chandran (m), the moon
Chandrani (f), wife of the moon
Chandranath (m), the moon
Chandraraj (m), moonbeam
Chandrima (f), the moon

Changuna (f), a good woman
Chapala (f), restless; lightning
Charita (f), good
Charuchandra (m), beautiful
Charulata (f), beautiful
Charumati (f), beautiful
Charuprabha (f), beautiful
Charusheela (f), a jewel
Charvi (f), a beautiful woman
Chatura (f), clever
Chaturbhuj (m), Lord Vishnu
Chetan (m), consciousness
Chetana (m), consciousness
Chhabi (f), picture
Chhandak (m), the charioteer of Lord Buddha
Chhaya (f), shadow
Chidananda (m), Lord Shiva
Chinmay (m), blissful
Chinmayi (f), blissful
Chinmayananda (m), blissful
Chintan, Chintana, Chintanika (f), meditation
Chirag (m), lamp
Chiranjeev (m), immortal
Chirantan (m), immortal
Chirayu (m), immortal
Chiti (f), love
Chitkala (f), knowledge
Chitra (f), picture; a star; name of a river
Chitrabhanu (m), fire
Chitral (m), of variegated colour
Chitralekha (f), beautiful design; a celestial maiden
Chitrali (f), a row of pictures
Chitramala (f), series of pictures
Chitrangada (f), one of Arjuna's wives
Chitrani (f), the river Ganga
Chitrarath (m), the sun
Chitrarekha (f), picture
Chitrasen (m), a king of Gandharvas
Chitrita (f), picturesque
Chitta (m), mind
Chittaranjan (m), joy of inner mind
Chittesh (m), lord of the soul

D

Dabeet (m), warrior
Daksha (f), the earth; Sati, wife of Shiva
Dakshata (f), skill
Dakshayani (f), Goddess Durga
Daman (m), one who controls
Damian (m), tamer
Damini (f), lightning
Damayanti (f), Nala's wife
Damodar (m), Lord Ganapati
Darpan (m), a mirror
Darpana (f), a mirror
Darshan (m), religious text
Dasharath (m), the father of Lord Rama
Dasharathi (m), Lord Rama
Daya (f), kindness
Dayamayee (f), kind
Dayanita (f), tender
Dayita (f), beloved
Debashis (m), benediction of god
Deeba (f), silk
Deenabandhu (m), friend of the poor
Deep (m), a lamp
Deepabali (f), row of lamps
Deepak (m), lustrous
Deepali (f), row of lamps
Deepan (m), lighting up
Deepanwita (f), lit by lamps
Deepankar (m), lord of light
Deepashikha (f), flame
Deependu (m), bright moon
Deepesh (m), lord of light
Deepika (f), a lamp
Deepit (m), lighted
Deepamala (f), row of lamps
Deepanwita (f), diwali
Deepaprabha (f), fully lighted
Deepta (f), shining
Deeptanshu (m), the sun
Deeptendu (m), bright moon
Deepti (f), flame; lustre
Deeptikana (f), a beam of light
Deeptiman (m), lustrous
Deeptimoy (m), lustrous
Deeptimoyee (f), lustrous
Dev (m), God; king
Devabrata (m), a name of Bhisma
Devadas (m), follower of God
Devahuti (f), daughter of Manu

Devajyoti (m), brightness of the Lord
Devak (m), divine
Devaki (f), mother of Krishna
Devangana (f), celestial maiden
Devapriya (f), dear to God
Devasree (f), divine beauty
Devendra (m), Lord Indra
Devdutta (m), king
Dev Kumar (m), son of gods
Devnarayan (m), king
Devnath (m), King of gods
Devesh (m), Lord Indra
Deveshwar (m), Lord Shiva
Devika (f), goddess
Devyani (f), daughter of Shukracharya
Dhananjay (m), Arjuna
Dhanashri (f), a raga
Dhanesh (m), lord of wealth
Dhanishta (f), a star
Dhanraj (m), Lord Kuber
Dhansukh (m), wealthy; happy
Dhanvant (m), wealthy
Dhanya (f), great
Dhara (f), the earth
Dharani (f), the earth
Dharanidhar (m), Shesh, the cosmic serpent
Dharitri (f), the earth
Dharmadas (m), one who serves his religion
Dharmanand (m), one who takes pleasure in his religion
Dharmamohan (m), one who is attracted by religion
Dharmendra (m), God of Dharma
Dharmendu (m), light of religion
Dharmpal (m), protector of his religion
Dharmveer (m), religious
Dhatri (f), Goddess Parvati
Dhawal (m), white
Dheeman (m), intelligent
Dheemant (m), wise; intelligent
Dheer (m), gentle
Dhiraj (m), emperor
Dheerendra (m), god of courage
Dhriti (f), patience
Dhritiman (m), patient
Dhruva (m), unshakeable; the Pole Star
Dhwani (m), sound
Dhyanesh (m), meditative
Diksha (f), initiation
Dilber (f), lover
Dilip (m), an ancestor of Lord Rama, a King
Dilshad (f), happy
Dilawar (m), brave

Dinanath (m), protector of the poor

Dinar (m), gold coin

Dindayal (m), kind to the poor

Dinesh (m), the sun

Disha (f), direction

Diti (f), wife of the sage Kashyap

Divakar (m), the sun

Divya (f), divine lustre

Divyanga (m), divine body

Divyendu (m), the moon

Doyel (f), a songbird

Draupadi (f), wife of the Pandavas

Dristi (f), eyesight

Drupad (m), a king, father of Draupadi

Dulal (m), dear one

Dulari (f), dear

Durga (f), succour; the Goddess

Durva, Durba (f), sacred grass

Dushyanta (m), a king from the epic Mahabharata; husband of Shakuntala

Dwaipayan (m), the sage Vyasa

Dwijaraj (m), king of Brahmins; the moon

Dwijendra (m), king of Brahmins; the moon

Dwijesh (m), king of Brahmins; the moon

Dwipavati (f), river

E

Ekanath (m), king

Ekavali (f), single-string necklace

Ekalavya (m), renowned for his devotion to his guru

Ekambar (m), sky

Ekata (f), unity

Ekaparna (f), wife of Himalaya

Ekram (m), honour

Ela (f), cardamom tree

Enakshi (f), dear-eyed

Esha (f), desire

Eshana (f), search

Eshita (f), one who desires

F

Faiyaz (m & f), artistic
Faiz (m), gain
Faiza (f), gain
Falak (m), the sky
Falguni, Phalguni (m & f), born in Falgun, a Hindu month; Arjun
Fanibhusan (m), Lord Shiva
Fanindra (m), the cosmic serpent Shesh
Fanishwar (m), lord of serpents, Vasuki
Fanish (m), the cosmic serpent Shesh
Faria (f), a caravan
Farha (f), happiness
Farhad (m), happiness
Farhat (m), happiness
Faraz (m), equitable
Farid (m), wide
Farida (f), turquoise
Farukh, Farokh (m), power of discrimination
Fateh (m), victory
Fatik (m), crystal
Fatima, Fatma (f), the Prophet Mohammad's daughter
Fawzia (f), successful
Firdaus (m), paradise
Firoz (m), name of a king
Firoza (f), turquoise
Fulki (f), spark
Fullara (f), wife of Kalketu
Foolan (f), flowering
Foolwati (f), delicate as a flower

See also entries under *P*

G

Gagan (m), sky
Gajanand (m), Lord Ganesh
Gajendra (m), the king of elephants
Gajra (f), a string of flowers
Gandhali (f), fragrance of flowers
Gandharva (m), celestial musician
Gandhik (m), fragrant
Ganesh (m), son of Lord Shiva & Parvati; elephant-headed god
Ganga (f), sacred river of India
Gangesh (m), Lord Shiva
Gangeya (m), of the Ganga
Gangika (f), river Ganga
Gangol (m), a precious stone
Ganapati (m), Lord Ganesh
Gargi (f), an ancient scholar
Gatita (f), a river
Gauhar (f), a pearl
Gaura (f), a fair woman
Gauranga (m), fair-bodied
Gaurav (m), honour
Gauri (f), a fair woman; Parvati
Gaurika (f), a young girl
Gaurinath (m), Lord Shiva
Gautam (m), Lord Buddha
Gautami (f), wife of sage Gautam; river Godavari
Gayatri (f), the chant of salvation; Goddess Durga
Gazala (f), a deer
Geena (f), silvery
Geet (m), song
Geeta (f), holy book of the advice of Lord Krishna to Arjuna
Geeti (f), a song
Geetika (f), a little song
Ghalib (m), excellent
Ghanashyam (m), Lord Krishna
Giri (m), mountain
Giridhar (m), Lord Krishna
Giridhari (m), Lord Krishna
Girija (f), born of a mountain; Goddess Parvati
Girik (m), Lord Shiva
Girilal (m), Lord Shiva
Girindra (m), Lord Shiva
Giriraj (m), lord of the mountains
Girish (m), Lord Shiva
Gitanjali (f), an offering of songs

Godavari (f), sacred river of India

Gokul (m), a place where Lord Krishna was brought up

Gomati (f), name of a river

Gool (f), a flower

Gopa (f), Gautama's wife

Gopal (m), Lord Krishna; protector of cows

Gopesh (m), Lord Krishna

Gopi (f), a cowherd; cowherd woman

Gopichand (m), name of a king

Gorakh (m), cowherd

Gorochana (f), Goddess Parvati

Gourishankar (m), Mt. Everest

Govinda (m), Lord Krishna

Govindi (f), a devotee of Lord Krishna

Gudakesha (m), the archer Arjuna

Gulab (f), rose

Gulfam (m), the colour of flowers

Gulzar (m), gardener

Gulzarilal (m), name of Lord Krishna

Gunjan (m), buzzing of a bee

Gunjana (f), buzzing of a bee

Gunwant (m), virtuous

Gunwanti (f), virtuous

Gupil (m), a secret

Gurdeep (m), light of the teacher

Gurjari (f), a raga

Gurpreet (m), love of the teacher

Guru (m), teacher

Gyan (m), knowledge

Gyanada (f), Goddess Saraswati

Gyandev (m), lord of knowledge

H

Habib (m), beloved
Habiba (f), beloved
Hafiz (m), protected
Hafiza (f), protected
Haimanti (f), born in the season of Hemanta
Haimavati (f), Parvati, Lord Shiva's wife
Hamid (m), friend
Hamir (m), a raga
Hanima (f), a wave
Hans (m), swan
Hansa (f), swan
Hansika (f), swan
Hansini (f), swan
Hanuman (m), the monkey god of Ramayana
Hanumant (m), the monkey god of Ramayana
Hardik (m), heartfelt
Harekrishna (m), Lord Krishna
Harendra (m), Lord Shiva
Haresh (m), Lord Krishna
Haridas (m), servant of Krishna
Harigopal (m), Lord Krishna
Harihar (m), Lord Vishnu and Shiva
Harikrishna (m), Lord Krishna
Harinakshi (f), doe-eyed
Harinarayan (m), Lord Vishnu
Harini (f), deer
Hariom (m), Lord Vishnu
Hariprasad (m), blessed by Lord Krishna
Haripriya (f), consort of Lord Vishnu; Lakshmi
Haritbaran (m), green
Hariram (m), Lord Rama
Harishankar (m), Lord Shiva
Harishchandra (m), King of Surya dynasty, charitable and upright
Harita (f), green
Harjeet (m), victorious
Harmendra (m), the moon
Haroon (m), hope
Harsh (m), happiness
Harsha (f), happiness
Harshad (m), giver of joy
Harshada (f), giver of joy
Harshavardhan (m), creator of joy
Harshil (m), joyful
Harshini (f), joyous
Harshit (m), joyous
Harshita (m), joyous
Hashmat (m), glory; joyful
Hasina (f), beautiful
Hasit (m), happy
Hasita (f), happy

Hassan (m), an Islamic saint
Hasumati (f), happy
Heer (m), diamond
Heera (f), diamond
Hem (m), gold
Hema (f), golden
Hemadri (m), the Himalaya
Hemanga (m), golden-bodied
Hemangi (f), golden-bodied
Hemanta (m), early winter
Hemanti (f), early winter
Hemendra (m), golden Lord
Hemendu (m), golden moon
Hemlata (f), golden creeper
Hemavati (f), golden Parvati
Hena (f), a flower
Heramba (m), Lord Ganesha
Hetal (f), friendly
Hima (f), snow
Himachal (m), the Himalayas
Himadri (m), Himalaya
Himaghna (m), the sun
Himani (f), snow
Himanish (m), Lord Shiva
Himanshu (m), the moon
Himmat (m), courage
Hina (f), henna
Hindola (f), a raga
Hiral (f), lustrous
Hiranya (m), gold
Hiranmay (m), golden
Hiranmayi (f), golden
Hirendra (m), lord of diamonds
Hirkani (f), small diamond
Hitendra (m), well-wisher
Hiya (f), heart
Hoor (f), a celestial beauty
Hriday (m), heart
Hridaynath (m), lord of the heart, beloved
Hrishikesh (m), Lord Vishnu
Husna (f), beautiful
Hussain (m), Islamic thinker, saint

I

Ibrahim (m), Abraham; earth
Idris (m), fiery Lord
Iha (f), the earth
Iham (m), expected
Ihina (f), enthusiasm
Ihit (m), prize; honour; respect
Ikshu (f), sugarcane
Imtiaz (m), power of discrimination
Imran (m), strong
Ila (f), wife of the sage Manu; the earth; water
Iman (m), name of a raga
Ina (f), mother
Inayat (f), kindness
Indira (f), Goddess Lakshmi
Indivar (m), blue lotus
Indrajeet (m), conqueror of Indra
Indrakanta (m), Lord Indra
Indraneel (m), sapphire
Indrani (f), wife of Lord Indra
Indrasena (f), daughter of King Nala
Indrayani (f), the name of a sacred river
Indubhushan (m), the moon
Induhasan (m), like a moon
Indukanta (m), like a moon
Indulal (m), moon's lustre
Indulekha (f), the moon
Indumati (f), the full moon
Indushekhar (m), like a moon
Induja (f), Narmada river
Intekhab (m), chosen
Irfan (m), knowledgeable
Ipsa (f), desire
Ipsita (f), desired
Iqbal (m), prosperity
Ira (f), earth; muse
Iravati (f), the river Ravi
Irshaad (m), signal
Isar (m), eminent; Lord Shiva
Isha (f), one who protects
Ishana (f), rich
Ishan (m), the Lord
Ishani (f), Parvati, wife of Lord Shiva
Ishika (f), paint brush
Ishita (f), mastery; wealth
Ishrat (m & f), affection
Ishwar (m), god
Ishwari (f), goddess
Ivy (f), a creeper
Izhar (m), submission

J

Jabeen (f), forehead
Jag (m), the universe
Jagadbandu (m), Lord Krishna
Jaganmay (m), spread over the universe
Jagannath (m), Lord Vishnu
Jagat (m), the universe
Jagadamba (f), mother of the universe
Jagadish (m), lord of the universe
Jagjeevan (m), worldly life
Jagriti (f), vigilance
Jahan (m), the world
Jahanara (f), queen of the world
Jaichand (m), victory of the moon
Jaidayal (m), victory of kindness
Jaidev (m), victory of God
Jaigopal (m), victory of Lord Krishna
Jaikrishna (m), victory of Lord Krishna
Jaimini (m), an ancient philosopher
Jainarayan (m), victory
Jainendra (m), conqueror of Indra
Jaipal (m), Lord Brahma
Jairaj (m), lord of victory
Jaisal (m), famous folk hero and singer
Jaishree (f), honour of victory
Jaisudha (f), nectar of victory
Jaisukh (m), joy of winning
Jaiwant (m), victory
Jaiwanti (f), victory
Jalabala (f), a river
Jalaja (f), lotus
Jalal (m), glory
Jalendu (m), moon in the water
Jalil (m), revered
Jamini (f), night
Jamuna (f), a holy river
Janak (m), father of Sita
Janaki (f), wife of Lord Rama; Sita
Janamejay (m), a mythological king
Janardan (m), Lord Vishnu
Janhavi (f), river Ganga
Japa (m), chanting
Japendra (m), lord of chants (Lord Shiva)
Japesh (m), lord of chants (Lord Shiva)
Jasbeer (m), victorious hero
Jashan (m), celebration
Jasoda (f), mother of Lord Krishna

Jasodhara (f), mother of Lord Buddha
Jaspal (m), Lord Krishna
Jaswant (m), famous
Jatan (m), nurturing
Jatin (m), pertaining to a saint
Javed (m), immortal
Jawahar (m), jewel
Jaya (f), Durga
Jayalakshmi (f), the goddess of victory
Jayalalita (f), victorious Goddess Durga
Jayamala (f), garland of victory
Jayanta (m), Lord Vishnu
Jayanti (f), Parvati
Jayantika (f), Goddess Durga; Parvati
Jayaprada (f), giver of victory
Jayati (f), victorious
Jayita (f), victorious
Jayashree (f), the goddess of victory
Jeemutbahan (m), Lord Indra
Jeeval (f), full of life
Jeevan (m), life
Jeevankala (f), art of life
Jeevanlata (f), creeper of life
Jehangir (m), Akbar's son

Jetashri (f), a raga

Jharna (f), a stream
Jhilmil (f), sparkling
Jhinuk (f), oyster
Jhoomer (m), ornament
Jigya (f), curiosity to know
Jignesh (m), curious to research
Jihan (m), the world
Jishnu (m), Arjuna
Jitendra (m), conqueror of Indra
Jivitesh (m), God
Jogindra, Joginder (m), Lord Shiva
Jograj (m), Lord Krishna
Jowaki (f), a firefly
Joshita (f), pleased
Joel (f), God
Jugnu (m), a firefly
Juhi (f), a flower
Jui (f), a flower
Juily (f), a flower
Jusal (m), pair
Jwalaprasad (m), gift of fire
Jyotibala (f), splendour
Jyotichandra (m), splendour
Jyotika (f), light; a flame
Jyotiprakash (m), splendour of the flame
Jyotiranjan (m), joyous flame

Jyotirdhar (m), holder of the flame
Jyotirmoy (m), lustrous
Jyotirmoyee (f), lustrous
Jyotishmati (f), lustrous
Jyotsna (f), moonlight

See also entries under *Y*

K

Kabir (m), name of a famous saint

Kadambari (f), Goddess Saraswati

Kadambini (f), an array of clouds

Kailas (m), abode of Lord Shiva

Kailashchandra (m), Lord Shiva

Kailashnath (m), Lord Shiva

Kaishori (f), Goddess Parvati

Kajal (f), kohl

Kajjali (f), kohl

Kakali (f), chirping of birds

Kala (f), art

Kalanidhi (f), treasure of art

Kalash (m), sacred pot

Kalavati (f), artistic

Kali (f), a bud; Parvati

Kalidas (m), a devotee of Goddess Kali

Kalika (f), a bud

Kalimohan (m), a devotee of Goddess Kali

Kalindi (f), the river Yamuna

Kalipada (m), a devotee of Goddess Kali

Kalicharan (m), a devotee of Goddess Kali

Kaliranjan (m), a devotee of Goddess Kali

Kallol (f), large waves; gurgling of water

Kalpana (f), imagination

Kalpita (f), the imagined

Kalyan (m), welfare

Kalyani (f), auspicious

Kamakshi (f), name of Goddess Lakshmi or Parvati; a girl with love-filled eyes

Kamal (m), lotus

Kamala (f), Goddess Lakshmi

Kamalakar (m), Lord Vishnu

Kamalakshi (f), one whose eyes are beautiful like lotuses

Kamalnayan (m), lotus-eyed

Kamalapati (m), Lord Vishnu

Kamalika (f), lotus

Kamalini (f), lotus

Kamalkali (f), the bud of a lotus

Kamana (f), desire

Kamini (f), a handsome woman

Kamod (m), a raga

Kamraj (m), cupid

Kamran (m), success

Kana (f), an atom
Kanad (m), an ancient philosopher
Kanak (f), gold
Kanakabati (f), a fairy-tale princess
Kanaklata (f), golden-creeper
Kanakpriya (f), lover of gold
Kanan (m & f), a garden; forest
Kananbala (f), nymph of the forest
Kanchan (m & f), gold
Kanchana (f), gold
Kanchi (f), a waistband
Kandarpa (m), Cupid
Kanha (m), Lord Krishna
Kanhaiya (m), Lord Krishna
Kanhaiyalal (m), Lord Krishna
Kanika (f), an atom
Kanishka (m), name of a king
Kankana (f), a bracelet
Kannan (f), Lord Krishna
Kanta (f), a beautiful woman
Kanti (f), lustre
Kantimoy (m), lustrous
Kantilal (m), lustrous
Kanu (m), Lord Krishna
Kanvar (m), young prince
Kanwal (m), lotus
Kanwaljeet (m), lotus
Kanwalkishore (m), lotus; Lord Krishna
Kapil (m), name of a sage
Kapila (f), name of the celestial cow
Kapish (m), Lord Hanuman
Kapotakshi (f), eyes like a pigeon's
Karabi (f), a flower
Karan (m), Karna, the firstborn of Kunti
Kareem (m), kind
Karna (m), the firstborn of Kunti
Kartar (m), master
Kartik (m), a Hindu month
Kartikeya (m), elder son of Lord Shiva
Karuna (f), compassion; mercy
Karunakar (m), merciful
Karunamay (m), merciful
Karunamayi (f), merciful
Karunashankar (m), merciful
Kashi (f), Varanasi, the holy city
Kashif (m), a connoisseur
Kashinath (m), Lord Shiva
Kashiprasad (m), blessed by Lord Shiva
Kashmira (f), from Kashmir

Kashyap (m) name of a sage
Kasturi (f), musk
Katyayani (f), Goddess Parvati
Kaumudi (f), moonlight
Kausar (m), lake of paradise
Kaushal (m), perfect
Kaushalya (f), mother of Rama
Kaushik (m), sage Vishwamitra
Kaustubh (m), a jewel of Lord Vishnu
Kaveri (f), a river
Kavi (m), a poet
Kaviraj (m) doctor
Kavita (f), a poem
Kedar (m), a raga
Kedarnath (m), Lord Shiva
Kesari (f), saffron; a lion
Keshav (m), Lord Vishnu
Keshika (f), a woman with beautiful hair
Keshini (f), a woman with beautiful hair
Ketaki (f), a monsoon flower
Ketan (m), home; banner
Ketana (f), a home
Kevalkumar (m), absolute
Kevalkishore (m), absolute
Keya (f), a monsoon flower
Keyur (m), armlet

Khadim (m), servant of God
Khajit (m), Lord Buddha
Khalid (m), immortal
Khazana (m), treasure
Khemchand (m), welfare
Khemprakash (m), welfare
Khushal (m), happy; safe
Khyati (f), fame
Kimaya (f), divine
Kinshuk (m), a flower
Kiran (m & f), ray of light
Kiranmay (m), full of light
Kiranmala (f), a garland of light
Kirit (m), a crown
Kirtana (f), praise
Kirti (f), fame
Kirtikumar (m), famous man
Kishore (m), young
Kishorekumar (m), young
Kishori (f), young
Kokila (f), the cuckoo
Komal (f), tender
Komala (f), tender
Koyel (f), the cuckoo
Krandasi (f), the sky and the earth
Kranti (f), revolution
Kripa (f), mercy
Kripal (m), merciful
Krishna (m), Lord Krishna
Krishna (f), Draupadi

Krishnachandra (m), Lord Krishna
Krishnadeva (m), Lord Krishna
Krishnakanta (m), Lord Krishna
Krishnakumar (m), Lord Krishna
Krishnalal (m), Lord Krishna
Krishnamurty (m), Lord Krishna
Krishnamurari (m), Lord Krishna
Krittika (f), the Pleiads
Krishanu (m), fire
Krishnakali (f), a flower
Krishnaroop (m), dark
Krishnendu (m), Lord Krishna
Kshama (f), forgiveness
Kshanika (f), momentary
Kshaunish (m), king
Kuber (m), god of wealth
Kuberchand (m), god of wealth
Kulbhushan (m), ornament of family
Kuldeep (m), light of family
Kularanjan (m), star of family
Kumar (m), prince
Kumari (f), unmarried woman
Kumkum (f), vermilion
Kumud (f), a lotus
Kumudini (f), a lotus
Kunal (m), son of emperor Ashok
Kundan (m), pure
Kundana (f), a flower
Kundanika (f), golden girl; a flower
Kundanlal (m), golden
Kunja (m), grove of trees
Kunjana (f), forest girl
Kunjabihari (m), Lord Krishna
Kunjalata (f), forest creeper
Kuntal (f), hair
Kuntala (f), a woman with luxurious hair
Kunti (f), the mother of the Pandavas
Kush (m), son of Lord Rama
Kushal (m), clever
Kusum (f), a flower
Kusumakar (m), spring
Kusumanjali (f), flower offering
Kusumavati (f), flowering
Kusumita (f), blooming
Kusumlata (f), flowering creeper

L

Labangalata (f), a flowering creeper
Laboni (f), grace
Lagan (m), appropriate time
Lajja (f), modesty
Lajjawati (f), a sensitive plant; modest woman
Lajwanti (f), a sensitive plant
Lajwati (f), modest
Lakshana (f), Duryodhana's daughter; one with auspicious signs on her
Laksha (f), white rose
Lakshmigopal (m), Lord Vishnu
Lakshman (m), younger brother of Rama
Lakshmi (f), goddess of wealth
Lakshmibanta (m), fortunate
Lakshmidhar (m), Lord Vishnu
Lakshmikanta (m), Lord Vishnu
Lakshmishree (f), fortunate appearance
Lalan (f), nurturing
Lalana (f), a beautiful woman
Lalima (f), redness
Lalataksha (m), Lord Shiva
Lalit (m), beautiful
Lalita (f), beautiful
Lalitkishore (m), beautiful
Lalitkumar (m), beautiful
Lalitmohan (m), beautiful
Lambodar (m), Lord Ganesha
Lankesh (m), Ravana
Lata (f), a creeper
Latafat (m), elegance
Latangi (f), a creeper
Latif (m), elegant
Latika (f), a small creeper
Lav (m), son of Lord Rama
Lavanya (f), grace
Leela (f), divine play
Leelamayee (f), playful
Leelavati (f), playful; Goddess Durga
Leena (f), devoted
Lekha (f), writing
Lily (f), a flower
Lipi (f), script
Lipika (f), a short letter
Lochan (m & f), the eye
Lohitaksha (m), Lord Vishnu
Lokesh (m), Lord Brahma
Loknath (m), Lord Vishnu
Lokranjan (m), Lord Vishnu
Lola (f), Goddess Lakshmi
Lopa (f), wife of sage Agastya
Lopamudra (f), wife of sage Agastya

M

Madan (m), Cupid
Madangopal (m), Lord Krishna
Madhav (m), Lord Krishna
Madhavdas (m), servant of Lord Krishna
Madhavi (f), a creeper with beautiful flowers; springtime
Madhu (m & f), honey
Madhul (f), sweet
Madhubala (f), sweet girl
Madhuchhanda (f), pleasing metrical composition
Madhuk (m), a honeybee
Madhukanta (m), the moon
Madhukar (m), honeybee
Madhuksara (f), one who showers honey
Madhulata (f), sweet creeper
Madhulekha (f), beautiful girl
Madhulika (f), honey
Madhumalati (f), a flowering creeper
Madhumati (f), full of honey
Madhumita (f), honey
Madhunisha (f), pleasant night
Madhup (m), a honeybee
Madhur (m & f), sweet
Madhura (f), sugar
Madhuri (f), sweetness
Madhurima (f), sweetness
Madhushri (f), the spring
Madhusudan (m), Lord Krishna
Madirakshi (f), woman with intoxicating eyes
Magan (m), engrossed
Megha (m), a star
Mahabahu (m), Arjuna
Mahadev (m), Lord Shiva
Mahadevi (f), Goddess Parvati
Mahagauri (f), Goddess Parvati
Mahalakshmi (f), Goddess Lakshmi
Mahamaya (f), Goddess Durga
Mahaniya (m), worthy of honour
Mahasweta (f), Goddess Saraswati
Mahati (f), great
Mahavir (m), a Jain prophet
Mahendra (m), Lord Vishnu
Mahesh (m), Lord Shiva
Maheshwar (m), Lord Shiva

Mahi (f), the earth
Mahika (f), the earth
Mahima (f), greatness
Mahin (m), kingly
Mahindra (m), a king
Mahipal (m), a king
Mahish (m), a king
Mahajabeen (f), beautiful
Mahjuba (f), a hostess
Mahmud (m), the Prophet of Islam
Mahtab (m), the moon
Mahua (f), an intoxicating flower
Maina (f), a bird
Mainak (m), a mountain; a Himalayan peak
Maithili (f), Sita
Maitreya (f), the name of a sage
Maitreyi (f), a learned woman of the past
Maitri (f), friendship
Makarand (m), a honeybee
Makshi (f), honeybee
Mala (f), a garland
Malashree (f), an early evening melody
Malati (f), a creeper with fragrant flowers
Malay (m), a mountain
Malaya (f), a creeper
Malhar (m), a raga
Malika (f), a garland
Malina (f), dark
Malini (f), a garland-maker
Mallika (f), jasmine
Mamata (f), affection
Manali (f), a bird
Manas (m), mind
Manasi (m), born of the mind
Manav (m), man
Manavendra (m), a king
Manda (f), a river
Mandakini (f), a river
Mandakranta (f), a Sanskrit metre
Mandar (m), a celestial tree
Mandarmalika (f), a garland of celestial flowers
Mandeep (m), light of the mind
Mandira (f), cymbals; home
Mangal (m), auspicious
Mangala (f), auspicious
Mangesh (m), Lord Shiva
Manohar (m), beautiful; captivating
Mani (m), a jewel
Manibhushan (m), supreme gem
Manideepa (f), a lamp of precious stones
Manik (m), ruby
Manikuntala (f), one whose hair is like gems

Manimala (f), a string of pearls
Manimekhala (f), a girdle of gems
Manindra (m), lord of the mind
Manish (m). intellect
Manisha, Monisha (f), intellect
Manishankar (m), Lord Shiva
Manjari (f), the sacred basil; blossom
Manjeet (m), conqueror of the mind
Manjira (f), ankle-bells
Manjistha (f), extremely beautiful
Manjyot (f), light of the mind
Manju (f), sweet
Manjubala (f), a sweet girl
Manjubhasa (f), Goddess Saraswati
Manjubhash (m), one whose speech is pleasing
Manjula (f), sweet
Manjulika (f), a sweet girl
Manjusha (f), treasure chest
Manjushri (f), sweet lustre
Manmatha (m), Cupid
Manmayi (f), jealous; Sri Radha
Manmohan (m), pleasing
Manoj (m), born of the mind
Manoranjan (m), pleasing
Manorama (f), beautiful
Mansukh (m), pleasing
Manu (m), original man
Mardav (m), softness
Marichi (f), name of a star
Markandeya (m), a devotee of Lord Shiva
Martanda (m), the sun
Marut (m), the wind
Maruti (m), Lord Hanuman
Maushmi (f), monsoon wind
Maya (f), illusion
Mayanka (m), the moon
Mayur (m), peacock
Mayura (f), illusion
Mayuri (f), peahen
Medha (f), intellect; Goddess Saraswati
Medini (f), the earth
Meena (f), precious blue stone
Meenakshi (f), a woman with beautiful eyes
Meera (f), a saintly woman
Megh (m), cloud
Meghal (f), cloud
Meghamala (f), array of clouds
Meghana (f), cloud
Meghashyam (m), Lord Krishna

Mehal (f), cloud
Mehboob (m), beloved
Mehbooba (f), beloved
Mehdi (m), a flower
Meher (f), benevolence
Mehmood (m), the Prophet of Islam
Mehrunissa (f), benevolent
Mehul (f), cloud; rain
Mekhala (f), girdle
Mena (f), wife of the Himalayas
Menaka (f), a celestial dancer
Mihir (m), the sun
Mihirkiran (m), ray of the sun
Milan (m), union
Milap (m), union
Milind (m), a bee
Milun (m), union
Minal (f), a precious stone
Minati (f), prayer
Mirium (f), wished-for child
Mirza (m), a prince
Misal (m), example
Mita (f), a friend
Mitali (f), friendship
Mithilesh (m), the king of Mithila, Janak, father of Sita
Mithun (m), Gemini
Mitra (m), friend; the sun
Mitul (m), friend

Mohajit (m), attractive
Mohak (m), attractive
Mohal (m), attractive
Mohamad (m), the Prophet of Islam
Mohan (m), Lord Krishna; attractive
Mohini (f), enchantress
Mohit (m), attracted
Mohita (m), attracted
Mohana (f), attractive
Mohnish (m), Lord Krishna
Mohul (m), attractive
Monisha (f), higher intelligence
Moti (m), pearl
Motilal (m), pearl
Moulik (m), valuable
Mridula (f), soft
Mriganayani (f), doe-eyed
Mriganka (m), the moon
Mrigankamouli (m), Lord Shiva
Mrigankasekhar (m), Lord Shiva
Mrigendra (m), lion
Mrigesh (m), lion
Mrinal (f), lotus
Mrinali (f), lotus
Mrinalini (f), lotus
Mrinmayi (f), of the earth
Mrityunjay (m), Lord Shiva
Mubarak (m), congratulations

Mudita (m), happy
Mudra (f), expression
Mudrika (f), ring
Mugdha (f), spellbound
Muhamad (m), the Prophet
Mukesh (m), Cupid
Mukta (f), liberated; pearl
Muktananda (m), liberated
Mukti (f), freedom from life and death
Mukul (m & f), bud
Mukunda (m), Lord Krishna
Mukut (m), crown
Mulkraj (m), king
Mumtaz (m), conspicuous
Muni (m), sage
Muniya (f), name of a bird
Murad (m), prowess
Murari (m), Lord Krishna
Murarilal (m), Lord Krishna
Murali (m), flute
Muralidhar (m), Lord Krishna
Muralimanohar (m), Lord Krishna
Musheer (m), advice

N

Naaz (f), pride
Nabarun (m), morning sun
Nabendu (m), new moon
Nabhi (m), focus; the best
Nachiketa (m), an ancient rishi, fire
Nachni (f), dancer; suggestive look
Nadir (m), pinnacle
Nadira (f), pinnacle
Nagendra (m), Seshnag
Nagesh (m), Seshnag
Nagina (f), jewel
Nahusha (m), a mythological king
Naina (f), name of a goddess
Nairit (m), south-west
Naishadh (m), King Nala, a hero from the Mahabharata who was King of Nishadha
Najma (f), sorry
Nakshatra (m), star
Nakul (m), name of one of the Pandavas
Nalin (m), lotus
Nalinaksha (m), lotus-eyed
Nalini (f), lotus
Naman (m), salutation
Namdev (m), Lord Vishnu
Namita (f), humble
Namrata (f), modesty

Nanak (m), guru of the Sikhs
Nand (m), joyful
Nanda (f), joyful
Nandan (m), pleasing
Nandana (f), daughter
Nandi (m), the bull of Shiva; Lord Shiva
Nandini (f), bestower of joy; Ganga; daughter
Nandita (f), happy
Naotau (m), new
Narayan (m), Lord Vishnu
Narayani (f), Goddess Lakshmi
Narendra (m), king
Narois (f), flower
Narahari (m), Lord Vishnu
Naresh (m), king
Narmada (f), a river
Narasimha (m), an incarnation of Lord Vishnu
Nartan (f) dance
Naseen (f), cool breeze
Natesh (m), Lord Shiva
Natun (f), new
Natwar (m), Lord Krishna
Naval (m), wonder
Naveen (m), new
Naveena (f), new
Navaneet (m), butter
Navaneeta (f), butter

Navrang (m), beautiful
Navroz (m), a Parsee festival
Nayan (m), eye
Nayana (f), lovely-eyed
Nayantara (f), iris
Nazima (f), song
Neela (f), blue
Neelabja (f), blue lotus
Neeladri (m), the Nilgiris
Neelakshi (f), blue-eyed
Neelam (f), sapphire
Neelambar (m), blue sky
Neelanjan (m), blue
Neelanjana (f), blue
Neelesh (m), Lord Krishna; moon
Neelkamal (f), blue lotus
Neelkanta (m), Lord Shiva
Neelmadhav (m), Lord Jagannath
Neelmani (m), sapphire
Neelotpal (m), blue lotus
Neepa (f), name of a flower
Neeraf (m), river
Neeraj (m), lotus; pearl
Neeraja (f), lotus, Goddess Lakshmi
Neeta (f), upright
Neeti (f), good behaviour
Neha (f), rain
Nehal (f), rainy; handsome
Netra (f), eye
Netravati (f), beautiful-eyed

Nibodh (m), knowledge
Nidhi (f), wealth
Nigam (m), treasure
Nihal (m), gratified
Nihar (m), dew
Niharika (f), nebula
Niket (m), home
Nikhat (m), fragrance
Nikhil (m), entire
Nikhilesh (m), lord of all
Nikhita (f), the earth
Nikunja (m), grove of trees
Nilasha (f), blueness
Nilay (m), home
Nilaya (f), home
Nileen (f), surrendered
Nilima (f), blueness
Niloufer (f), a celestial being
Nimai (m), Chaitanya
Nimish (m), split-second
Nina (f), lovely-eyed
Ninad (m), sound
Nipun (m), expert
Nirad (m), cloud
Nirajit (m), illuminated
Niramay (m), without blemish
Niramayi (f), without blemish
Niranjan (m), unblemished Lord Shiva
Niranjana (f), name of a river; Goddess Durga; the night of the full moon

Nirav (m), quiet
Nirbhay (m), fearless
Nirjhar (m), waterfall
Nirmal (m), pure
Nirmala (f), pure
Nirmalya (m), flower offered to Gods
Nirmit (m), created
Nirmohi (m), unattached
Nirupam (m), without comparison
Nirupama (f), without comparison
Nirvan (m), liberation
Nischal (m), calm
Nisha (f), night
Nishanath (m), moon
Nishad (m), seventh note of the octave
Nishant (m), dawn
Nishesh (m), entire
Nishikanta (m), the moon
Nishita (f), sharp
Nishith (m), night
Nishithini (f), night
Nishok (m), happy
Nishtha (f), devotion
Nissim (m), unbounded
Nitin (m), master of the right path
Nitish (m), master of the right path
Nitya (f), constant
Nityagopal (m), Lord Krishna
Nityananda (m), Lord Krishna; always happy
Nityapriya (m) ever-pleasing
Nivedita (f), surrendered (to God)
Nivritti (f), non-attachment
Niyati (f), fate
Noopur (f), anklet
Noor (f), light
Noorjehan (f), light of the world
Nripa (m), king
Nripesh (m), king of kings
Nusrat (f), help
Nutan (f), new

O

Ojal (f), vision
Ojas (m), lustre
Ojaswini (f), lustrous
Om (m), the sacred syllable
Omana (f), a woman
Omar (m), an era
Omja (m), born of cosmic unity
Omkar (m), the sound of the sacred syllable
Omprakash (m), light of God
Omrao, Umrao (m), king
Omswaroop (m), manifestation of divinity
Osman, Usman (m), slave of God

P

Paavan (m), purifier
Padma (f), Goddess Lakshmi
Padmaja (f), Lakshmi
Padmakali (f), lotus bud
Padmal (f), lotus
Padmalaya (f), lake of lotuses
Padmalochana (f), lotus-eyed
Padman (m), lotus
Padmanabha (m), Lord Vishnu
Padmapati (m), Lord Vishnu
Padmavati (f), Goddess Lakshmi
Padmini (f), lotus
Pakhi (f), bird
Pakshi (f), bird
Palak (m), eyelash
Palash (m), a flowering tree
Palashkusum (m), the flower of Palash
Palashranjan (m), beautiful like a Palash
Pallab (m), new leaves
Pallavi (f), new leaves
Pallavini (f), with new leaves
Panchali (f), Draupadi's name
Panchanan (m), Lord Shiva
Pandhari (m), Lord Vithobha
Panduranga (m), Lord Vithobha
Pankaj (m), lotus
Pankaja (f), lotus
Panna (f), emerald
Pannalal (m), emerald
Paravasu (m), name of a sage
Parag (m), pollen
Param (m), the best
Parama (f), exceeding; the best
Parameshwar (m), Almighty Lord
Parameshwari (f), Goddess Durga
Paramhansa (m), supreme soul
Paramita (f), wisdom
Paranjay (m), Varun; Lord of the Sea
Parantapa (m), conqueror; Arjuna
Paras (m), touchstone
Parashar (m), an ancient sage
Parasmani (m), touchstone
Paresh (m), supreme Lord
Pari (f), fairy
Paridhi (f), realm
Parijat (m), a celestial flower

Parikshit (m), name of an ancient king
Parimal (m), fragrance
Paritosh (m), satisfaction
Paramananda (m), superlative joy
Paramesh (m), Lord Shiva
Parnad (m), a Brahmin in the epics
Parnal (f), leafy
Parnashri (f), leafy beauty
Parni (f), leafy
Parnika (f), creeper
Parashuram (m), sixth incarnation of Lord Vishnu
Partha (m), Arjuna
Parthapratim (m), like Arjuna
Parthivi (f), Sita
Parul (f), name of a flower
Parvani (f), full moon; a festival or a special day
Parvati (f), Durga
Parvatinandan (m), Lord Ganesh
Parveen (f), star
Parvesh (m), Lord of celebration
Pasupati (m), Lord Shiva
Patakin (m), holder of a banner
Patamanjari (f), a raga
Patanjali (m), famous Yoga philosopher
Pathik (m), a traveller

Pathin (m), traveller
Patralekha (f), a name from ancient epics
Patralika (f), new leaves
Pavak (m), fire
Pavan (m), breeze
Pavani (m), Hanuman
Pavani (f), sacred; river Ganga
Pavitra (m), pure
Payal (f), anklet
Payas (m), water
Payod (m), cloud
Payoja (f), lotus
Peeyush (m), nectar
Phanindra (m), Sesh; the divine snake
Phiroza (f), turquoise
Phoolan (f), flower
Pia (f), beloved
Piki (f), cuckoo
Pinaki (m), Lord Shiva
Pingala (f), Lakshmi
Pirmohammed (m), the holy prophet
Pitambar (m), Lord Vishnu
Piyali (f), a tree
Piyush (m), nectar
Pival (f), a tree
Pooja (f), worship
Poojan (m), worship
Poojit (m), worshipped
Poonam (f), merit
Poorbi (f), eastern
Poorna (m), complete

Poornachandra (m), full moon
Poushali (f), of the month Poush
Prabal (m), coral
Prabha (f), lustre
Prabhakar (m), the sun
Prabhas (m), lustrous
Prabhat (m), morning
Prabhati (f), of the morning
Prabhav (m), effect
Prabodh (m), consolation
Prabuddha (m), awakened
Prachetas (m), energy
Prachi (f), east
Prachur (m), abundant
Pradeep (m), lamp
Pradeepta (f), glowing
Pradosh (m), dusk
Pradyot (m), lustre
Pradyumna (m), cupid
Pradyun (m), radiant
Praful (m), blooming
Prafulla (m), blooming
Pragati (f), progress
Pragun (m), straight; honest
Pragya (f), wisdom
Pragyaparamita (f), wise
Pragyawati (f), a wise woman
Prahlad (m), joy
Prajesh (m), Lord Brahma
Prajin (m), kind
Prajit (m), kind
Prakat (m), manifested
Prakash, Parkash (m), light
Prakriti (m), nature
Prama (f), knowledge of truth
Pralay (m), Himalay
Pramada (f), woman
Pramila (f), one of Arjuna's wives
Pramiti (f), knowledge of truth
Pramod (m), delight
Pran (m), life
Pranati (f), prayer
Pranav (m), the sacred syllable, Om
Pranay (m), love
Pranit (m), modest
Pranjal (m), simple; uncomplicated
Pranjivan (m), life
Pransukh (m), joy of life
Prapti (f), gain
Prarthana (f), prayer
Prasad (m), blessing
Prasanna (m), happy
Prasenjit (m), a king in the epics
Prasham (m), peace
Prashansa (f), praise
Prashanta (m), calm
Prashanti (f), peace
Prasun (m), blossom
Pratap (m), glory

Prateep (m), king Shantanu's father
Prateet (m), manifested
Pratibha (f), keen intellect
Pratik (m), symbol
Pratima (f), image
Pratishtha (f), pre-eminence
Pratiti (m), faith; understanding
Pratul (m), plenty
Praval (m), fierce, strong
Praver (m), chief
Praveen (m), expert, experienced
Pravir (m), brave
Prayag (m), confluence
Preeti (f), love
Prem (f), love
Prema (f), love
Premala (f), loving
Premendra (m), lover
Prerana (f), encouragement
Preyasi (f), beloved
Prita (f), dear one
Pritam (m), beloved
Pritha (f), Kunti, mother of Pandavas
Prithu (m), a king from the epics
Prithvi (m), earth
Prithviraj (m), king of the earth
Pritika (f), dear one
Pritikana (f), an atom of love
Pritilata (f), a creeper of love
Priya (m), beloved
Priyabrata (m), devoted to pleasing
Priyadarshini (f), lovely
Priyal (f), beloved
Priyam (f), beloved
Priyamvada (f), sweet-spoken
Priyanka (f), dear one
Priyasha (f), dear one
Puja (f), worship
Pujit (m), worshipped
Pujita (f), worshipped
Pukhraj (m), topaz
Pulak (m), joy
Pulakesh (m), joyous
Pulastya (m), an ancient sage
Pulin (m), beautiful
Pulish (m), name of a sage
Puloma (f), wife of the sage Bhrigu
Punam (f), full moon
Punarnava (f), a star
Pundalik (m), lotus
Pundarik (m), lotus
Punit (m), pure
Punita (f), pure
Punyabrata (m), dedicated to the good

Punyasloka (m), sacred verse
Purandar (m), Lord Indra
Puranjay (m), Lord Shiva
Puravi, Porabi (f), a raga
Purna (f), fulfilled
Purnananda (m), God
Purnendu (m), full moon
Purnima (f), full moon
Puru (m), abundant; name of a king
Pururava (m), the founder of Chandra dynasty
Purushottam (m), Lord Vishnu
Purva (f), elder
Purvaja (f), elder sister
Pushkar (m), lotus ; a lake
Pushpa (f), flower
Pushpak (m), mythical vehicle of Lord Vishnu
Pushpanjali (f), flower offering
Pushpita (f), decorated with flowers
Putul (f), doll
Pyarelal (m), Lord Krishna
Pyaremohan (m), Lord Krishna

Q

Quamar (m), the moon
Quarratulain (f), God's mercy

Quasar (f), meteor
Quasim (m), old generation
Qutub (m), tall

R

Raakhi (f), symbol of protection; full moon in the month of Sravan
Rabia (f), famous; godly
Rachana (f), creation
Rachita (f), created
Radha (f), the beloved of Lord Krishna
Radhakanta (m), Lord Krishna
Radhakrishna (m), Radha and Lord Krishna
Radhavallabh (m), Lord Krishna (beloved of Radha)
Radheshyam (m), Lord Krishna
Radheya (m), Karna
Radhika (f), Radha
Rafat (m), elevation
Raghav (m), Lord Rama
Raghavendra (m), Lord Rama
Raghu (m), the family of Lord Rama
Raghunath (m), Lord Rama
Raghunandan (m), Lord Rama
Raghupati (m), Lord Rama
Raghuvir (m), Lord Rama
Ragini (f), a melody
Rahas (m), secret
Raheem (m), merciful
Rahman (m), merciful
Rahul (m), son of Lord Buddha
Raj (m), kingdom
Raja (m), king
Rajalakshmi (f), Goddess Lakshmi
Rajam (m), Goddess Lakshmi
Rajan (m), king
Rajani (f), night
Rajanigandha (f), a flower
Rajas (m), mastery; fame; pride
Rajat (m), silver
Rajata (f), sovereignty
Rajatshubhra (m), white as silver
Rajdulari (f), dear princess
Rajendra (m), king
Rajendramohan (m), king
Rajesh (m), king
Rajeshwari (f), Goddess Parvati
Rajhans (f), swan
Rajendrakumar (m), king
Rajit (m), decorated
Rajiv (m), lotus
Rajivlochan (m), Lord Vishnu
Rajivnayan (m), Lord Vishnu
Rajkumari (f), princess

Rajnandini (f), princess
Rajanikanta (m), moon
Rajarshi (m), sagelike king
Rajrishi (m), sagelike king
Rajshri (f), royalty's lustre
Rajyeshwar (m), king
Raka (f), full moon
Rakesh (m), the moon
Raksha (f), protection
Ram (m), Lord Rama; one who pleases
Rama (f), Goddess Lakshmi
Ramakanta (m), Lord Vishnu
Raman (m), cupid
Ramani (f), woman
Ramanuja (m), Lord Krishna
Ramashray (m), Lord Vishnu; protected by Rama
Ramavatar (m), Lord Rama
Rambha (f), celestial dancer
Ramchandra (m), Lord Rama
Ramesh (m), Lord Vishnu
Rameshwar (m), Lord Shiva
Ramita (f), pleasing
Ramkishore (m), Lord Rama
Ramkrishna (m), Lord Rama and Lord Krishna
Ramkumar (m), Lord Rama
Rammohan (m), Lord Rama
Ramnath (m), Lord Rama
Ramprasad (m), Lord Rama
Rampratap (m), Lord Rama
Ramratan (m), Lord Rama
Ramswaroop (m), Lord Rama
Ramya (f), beautiful
Randhir (m), brave
Rangan (m), a flower
Rangana (f), one who gives pleasure
Ranganath (m), Lord Vishnu
Rani (f), queen
Ranita (f), tinkling
Ranjan (m), entertaining
Ranjana (f), delightful
Ranajay (m), victorious
Ranajit (m), victorious
Ranjit (m), victorious
Ranjita (f), adorned
Rasbihari (m), Lord Krishna
Rasesh (m), Lord Krishna
Rashi (f), collection
Rashmi (f), sunlight
Rasna (f), the tongue
Rashmika (f), ray of light
Rasik (m), connoisseur

Rasika (f), connoisseur
Rasaraj (m), mercury
Rasul (m), angel
Ratan (m), precious stone
Rathin (m), celestial charioteer
Rati (f), consort of cupid
Ratish (m), cupid
Ratna (f), precious stone
Ratnali (f), a jewelled necklace
Ratnabala (f), jewelled
Ratnabali (f), string of pearls
Ratnakar (m), ocean
Ratnajyoti (f), lustrous jewel
Ratnalekha (f), splendour of jewels
Ratnamala (f), string of pearls
Ratnangi (f), jewel-bodied
Ratnaprabha (f), lustrous jewel
Ratnapriya (f), lover of jewels
Ratul (m), sweet
Ravi (m), sun
Ravinandan (m), Karna
Ravindra (m), sun
Raviprabha (f), light of the sun
Ravishu (m), cupid
Raza (m), hope
Razak (m), devotee

Rebanta (m), a son of Surya
Rehman (m), merciful
Rehmat (m), mercy
Rekha (f), line; artwork
Renu (f), atom
Renuka (f), the mother of Parasuram, the sixth incarnation of Lord Vishnu
Resham (f), silk
Reshma (f), silken
Reshmi (f), silken
Reva (f), a star
Revati (f), a star
Riddhi (f), good fortune
Riddhiman (m), possessed of good fortune
Riju (f), innocent
Rijul (m), innocent
Rijuta (f), innocence
Ripudaman (m), killer of enemies
Rishabh (m), second note of octave
Rishi (m), sage
Rishika (f), saintly
Rishikesh (m), Lord Vishnu
Riti (f), memory; well-being
Ritu (f), season
Rituraj (m), spring
Ritvik (m), priest
Riyaz (m), practice

Rizvan (m), harbinger of good news
Rochak (m), tasty
Rochan (m), bright
Rohan (m), ascending
Rohanlal (m), Lord Krishna
Rohini (f), a star
Rohit (m), red
Rohitasva (m), son of King Harishchandra
Roma (f), Lakshmi
Ronak (m), embellishment
Roshan (m), illumination
Roshni (f), brightness
Rubaina (f), bright
Ruchi (f), lustre; beauty
Ruchir (m), beautiful
Ruchira (f), beautiful
Rudra (m), Lord Shiva
Rudrapriya (f), Goddess Durga
Rukma (f), golden
Rukmini (f), consort of Lord Krishna
Ruksana (f), brilliant
Ruma (f), wife of Sugriva
Rupa (f), silver
Rupak (m), beautiful
Rupali (f), beautiful
Rupashi (f), beautiful
Rupashri (f), beautiful
Rushil (m), charming
Rustom (m), warrior

S

Sachet (m), consciousness
Sachetan (m), animated
Sacchidananda (m), total bliss
Sachi (f), wife of Lord Indra
Sachin (m), Lord Indra
Sachit (m), consciousness
Sadaf (f), pearl
Sadananda (m), eternal bliss
Sadashiva (m), eternally pure
Sadeepan (m), lighted up
Sadgati (f), liberation
Sadguna (f), good virtues
Sadhan (f), fulfilment
Sadhana (f), worship
Sadhvi (f), virtuous woman
Sadhika (f), achiever
Sadiq (m), kingly
Sadiqua (f), kindly
Saeed (m), priestly
Saeeda (f), priestly
Safia (f), chaste
Sagar (m), ocean
Sagarika (f), wave; born in the ocean
Sagun (m), possessed of good qualities
Saguna (f), possessed of good qualities
Sahaj (m), natural
Sahana (f), a raga
Sahas (m), bravery
Sahdev (m), one of the Pandava princes
Saheli (f), friend
Sahib (m), the lord
Sahiba (f), the lady
Sahil (m), guide
Sahila (f), guide
Sai (f), a flower
Sainath (m), Saibaba
Saiprasad (m), blessing of Saibaba
Saipratap (m), power of Saibaba
Sajal (m), moist
Sajala (f), clouds
Sajan (m), beloved
Sajili (f), decorated
Sajni (f), beloved
Saket (m), Lord Krishna
Sakhi (f), friend
Sakina (f), friend
Salarjung (m), beautiful
Saleem (m), healthy; simple
Salena (f), the moon
Salil (m), water
Salila (f), water
Salim (m), happy; peaceful

Salima (f), happy; peaceful
Salma (f), peace
Salman (m), high
Samar (m), war
Samarendra (m), Lord Vishnu
Samarendu (m), Lord Vishnu
Samarjit (m), Lord Vishnu
Samarth (m), powerful
Samata (f), equality
Sambaran (m), restraint; name of an ancient king
Sambhav (m), born; manifested
Sambit (m), consciousness
Sambuddha (m), wise
Sameena (f), happy
Samendra (m), winner of war
Sameen (m), valuable
Sameer (m), breeze
Samhita (f), a vedic composition
Samidha (f), an offering for a sacred fire
Samiksha (f), overview
Samir (m), breeze
Samiran (m), breeze
Samit (f), collected
Samita (f), collected
Sampada (f), wealthy
Sampat (m), prosperous
Sampatti (f), wealth
Sampriti (f), attachment
Samudra (m), ocean
Samudragupta (m), a famous Gupta king
Samudrasen (m), lord of the ocean
Samyak (m), enough
Sana (f), praise, prayer
Sanabhi (m), related
Sanam (m), beloved
Sananda (f), happy
Sanat (m), Lord Brahma
Sanatan (m), eternal
Sanchali (f), movement
Sanchay (m), collection
Sanchaya (f), collection
Sanchit (m), collected
Sanchita (f), collection
Sandeepan (m), a sage
Sandhya (f), evening
Sandip (f), beautiful
Sangita (f), musical
Saniya (f), moment
Sanjana (f), gentle
Sanjay (m), Dhritarashtra's charioteer
Sanjiv (m), love; life
Sanjivan (m), immortality
Sanjivani (f), immortality
Sanjukta (f), wife of king Prithviraj
Sanjula (f), beautiful
Sanjushree (f), beautiful
Sankalpa (m), resolve

Sankarshan (m), a name of Balaram, brother of Lord Krishna
Sanket (m), signal
Sankul (f), full of
Sannidhi (f), nearness
Sanobar (m), palm tree
Sanvali (f), dusky
Sanskriti (f), culture
Santawana (f), consolation
Santayani (f), of the evening
Santosh (m), contentment
Sanwari (f), dusky
Sanwariya (m), Lord Krishna
Sanyog (m), coincidence
Sanyukta (f), joined; united
Sapan (m), dream
Saparna (f), leafy
Saquib (m), bright
Sarada (f), Goddess Saraswati
Sarakshi (f), good sight
Saral (m), straight
Sarala (f), straight; honest
Sarama (f), wife of Bibhisan
Saranya (f), surrendered
Saras (m), a bird; lake
Sarasi (f), lake
Sarasija (m), lotus
Saraswati (f), Goddess of learning
Sarat (m), a sage
Sarayu (f), a holy river
Sarbajit (m), one who has conquered everything
Sarbani (f), Goddess Durga
Sarfaraz (m), head held high
Sarika (f), a koel
Sarit (f), river
Sarjana (f), creative; creation
Saroj (m & f), lotus
Saroja (f), lotus
Sarojini (f), lotus
Sartaj (m), crown
Sarthak (m), well done
Sarup (m), beautiful
Saruprani (f), beautiful woman
Sarvadaman (m), son of Shakuntala (Bharat)
Sarvesh (m), lord of all
Sarwar (m), promotion
Sashreek (m), prosperous
Sasmita (f), smiling
Satyavati (f), truthful
Sati (f), chaste woman
Satindra (m), Lord Vishnu
Satish (m), victorious
Satrajit (m), father of Satyabhama, wife of Lord Krishna
Satya (f), truth
Satyajit (m) wedded to truth

Satyakam (m), son of Jabala in the Mahabharata
Satyaki (m), charioteer of Krishna
Satyamohan (m), truthful
Satyananda (m), joy of truth
Satyanarayan (m), Lord Krishna
Satyankar (m), true; good
Satyapraksh (m), light of truth
Satyapriya (m), devoted to truth
Satyarupa (f), truth personified
Satyasheel (m), truthful
Satyavan (m), husband of Savitri; true
Satyavati (f), truthful
Satyavrata (m), dedicated to truth
Satyendra (m), lord of truth
Saudamini (f), lightning
Savar (m), Lord Shiva
Savita (f), the sun
Savitashri (f), lustre of the sun
Savitendra (m), the sun
Savitri (f), a river; Goddess Saraswati
Savyasachi (m), Arjuna
Sawan (m), a Hindu month
Sawini (f), a river

Sayam (m), evening
Sayed (m), leader
Sayeeda (f), leader
Seema (f), boundary
Seemanta (m), parting line of hair
Seemanti (f), parting line of hair
Seemantini (f), woman
Seerat (f), inner beauty; fame
Sejal (f), river water
Selma (f), fair
Semanti (f), a white rose
Serena (f), quiet
Sevabrata (m), dedicated to serving others
Sevak (m), servant
Sevati (f), white rose
Sevita (f), cherished
Shaan (m), pride
Shabab (f), beauty
Shabana (f), decorated
Shabari (f), a tribal devotee of Lord Rama
Shabnum (f), dew
Shachi (f), wife of Lord Indra
Shachin(dra) (m), Lord Indra
Shadab (m), fresh
Shagufta (f), flowering
Shaheen (m), tender
Shaheena (f), tender
Shahid (m), patriot

Shaibalini (f), a mossy river
Shaila (f), Goddess Parvati
Shailendra (m), king of mountains
Shailesh (m), king of mountains
Shaili (f), style
Shaistakhan (m), polite
Shakambari (f), Goddess Parvati
Shakib (m), patience
Shakeel (f), handsome
Shakeela (f), beautiful
Shakila (m), beautiful
Shakti (f), Goddess Durga; power
Shaktidhar (m), Lord Shiva
Shakuntala (f), brought up by birds
Shakyasinha (m), Lord Buddha
Shalaka (f), Goddess Parvati
Shalin (f), silk-cotton tree
Shalini (f), modest
Shalmali (f), silk-cotton tree
Shama (f), a flame
Shambhavi (f), Goddess Parvati
Shambhu (m), Lord Shiva
Shameek (m), an ancient sage
Shami (m), fire
Shamim (f), fragrance
Shamindra (m), quiet; gentle
Shameena (f), beautiful
Shamita (f), peacemaker
Shampa (f), lightning
Shams (m), fragrance
Shamshad (m), beautiful tree
Shandar (m), proud
Shankar (m), Lord Shiva
Shankari (f), Goddess Parvati
Shankha (m), conch
Shankhamala (f), a fairytale princess
Shanmukha (m), Kartikeya, first son of Lord Shiva
Shanta (f), peaceful; daughter of King Dasarath
Shantala (f), Goddess Parvati
Shantanu (m), a king from the epic Mahabharata
Shantashil (m), gentle
Shanti (f), peace
Shantimay (m), peaceful
Shantinath (m), lord of peace
Shantiprakash (m), light of peace
Shantipriya (m), peace-loving
Sharad, Sarat (m), autumn

Sharadchandra (m), autumn moon

Sharadindu (m), autumn moon

Sharadini (f), autumn

Sharan (m), shelter

Sharang (m), deer

Sharankumari (f), shelter

Sharanya (f), surrender

Shardul (m), tiger

Shariq (m), intelligent

Sharmila (f), happy

Sharmistha (f), wife of Yayati

Sharvani (f), Goddess Parvati

Sharvari (f), the night

Shashanka (m), the moon

Shashadhar (m), the moon

Shashi (f), the moon

Shashibala (f), the moon

Shashibhushan (m), Lord Shiva

Shashikiran (m), moon's rays

Shashimohan (m), the moon

Shashirekha (f), moon's ray

Shashishekhar (m), Lord Shiva

Shaswati (f), eternal

Shatarupa (f), Lord Brahma's wife

Shatrunjay (m), victorious over enemies

Shatrughna (m), victorious over enemies

Shatrujit (m), victorious over enemies

Shaukat (m), grand

Shaunak (m), a great sage

Sheela (f), of gentle disposition

Sheetal (m), cool

Sheetala (f), cool

Shefali (f), a flower

Shefalika (f), a flower

Shejali (f), a fruit

Shekhar (m), Lord Shiva

Shesh (m), a cosmic serpent

Shishirchandra (m), winter moon

Shishirkana (f), particles of dew

Shevanti (f), a flower

Shevantilal (m), a crysanthemum

Shibani (f), Goddess Durga

Shikha (m), flame

Shikhar (m), peak

Shilavati (f), a river

Shilpa (f), well-proportioned

Shilpita (f), well-proportioned

Shipra (f), a river

Shirin (f), sweet

Shirish (m), a flower; raintree

Shiromani (m), superb jewel

Shishir (m), winter
Shishirkumar (m), the moon
Shishupal (m), son of Subhadra
Shiuli (f), a flower
Shiv (m), Lord Shiva
Shivangi (f), beautiful body
Shivani (f), Goddess Parvati
Shivendra (m), Lord Shiva
Shivendu (m). pure moon
Shivesh (m), Lord Shiva
Shivlal (m), Lord Shiva
Shivraj (m), Lord Shiva
Shivshankar (m), Lord Shiva
Shobhita (f), splendid
Shobha (f), splendour
Shobhan (m), splendid
Shobhana (f), beautiful
Shoorsen (m), brave
Shorashi (f), young woman
Shraddha (f), veneration
Shravan (m), name of a Hindu month
Shravana, Shrabana (f), name of a star
Shravankumar (m), a character from the epic Ramayana
Shravani (f), born in the month of Shravan
Shravanti (f), a name in Buddhist literature
Shravasti (f), an ancient Indian city
Shree (f), Goddess Lakshmi
Shreela (f), beautiful
Shreemayi (f), fortunate
Shreeparna (f), tree adorned with leaves
Shrenik (m), organised
Shreshta (m), the best
Shreya (f), better
Shreyas (m), good
Shreyashi (f), good
Shridevi (f), goddess
Shri (f), lustre
Shrilata (f), lustrous creeper
Shrilekha (f), lustrous essay
Shridhar (m), Lord Vishnu
Shridula (f), blessing
Shrigauri (f), Goddess Parvati
Shrigeeta (f), the sacred Geeta
Shrigopal (m), Lord Krishna
Shrihari (m), Lord Krishna
Shrijani (f), creative
Shrikanta (m), beautiful
Shrikirti (f), lustrous fame
Shrikrishna (m), Lord Krishna
Shrikumar (m), beautiful
Shrikumari (f), lustrous girl

Shrimati (f), Goddess Lakshmi; fortunate
Shrimayi (f), fortunate
Shrinath (m), Lord Vishnu
Shrinivas (m), Lord Vishnu
Shripad (m), Lord Vishnu
Shripal (m), Lord Vishnu
Shripati (m), Lord Vishnu
Shriram (m), Lord Rama
Shriranga (m), Lord Vishnu
Shrish (m), Lord Vishnu
Shrivalli (f), Goddess Lakshmi
Shrivatsa (m), Lord Vishnu
Shriyans (m), wealth
Shruti (f), hearing; Vedic text
Shubha (m), auspicious
Shubhada (f), giver of luck
Shubhang (m), handsome
Shubhangi (f), handsome
Shubhankar (m), auspicious
Shubhashis (m), blessing
Shubhendu (m), lucky moon
Shubhra (f), white; the Ganga
Shubhranshu (m), the moon
Shuchismita (f), one who has a pure smile
Shuchita (f), purity
Shuddhashil (m), well-born
Shukla (f), white; Goddess Saraswati
Shukti (f), pearl-oyster
Shulka (f), Goddess Saraswati
Shweta (f), white
Shyam (m), Lord Krishna
Shyama (f), dark as cloud; Goddess Kali
Shyamal (f), dusky
Shyamala (f), dusky
Shyamalendu (m), dusky
Shyamali (f), dusky
Shyamalika (f), dusky
Shyamalima (f), dusky beauty
Shyamasri (f), dusky beauty
Shyamari (f), dusky
Shyamlata (f), a creeper with dusky leaves
Shyamsundar (m), Lord Krishna
Shyla (f), Goddess Parvati
Sibani (f), Goddess Parvati
Siddhanta (m), principle
Siddhartha (m), a name of Lord Buddha
Siddheshwar (m), Lord Shiva
Siddheshwari (f), a goddess
Siddhi (f), achievement
Siddhima (f), achievement
Sikata (f), sand
Sikta (f), wet
Simrit, Smrita (f), remembered

Simran, Smaran (f), remembrance
Sindhu (f), ocean; river Sindhu
Sinsapa (f), Ashok tree
Siraj (m), lamp
Sita (f), wife of Lord Rama
Sitakanta (m), Lord Rama
Sitanshu (m), the moon
Sitara (f), a star
Sitikantha (m), Lord Shiva
Sivanta (m), Lord Shiva
Siya (f), Sita
Smaran (m), remembrance
Smarajit (m), one who has conquered lust
Smita (f), smiling
Smriti (f), memory
Smritiman (m), unforgettable
Smritirekha (f), memory
Sneha (f), affection
Snehal (f), friendly
Snehalata (f), creeper of love
Snehanshn (m), affectionate
Snehin (m), a friend
Snigdha (f), soft
Sohail (m), moon-glow
Sohaila (f), moon-glow
Soham (m), "I am He"—the presence of divinity in each soul
Sohan (m), charm
Sohil (m), beautiful
Sohni (f), beautiful
Som (m), the moon
Soma (f), moon-rays
Somalakshmi (f), lustre of the moon
Somendra (m), moon
Somansh (m), half moon
Someshwar (m), Lord Shiva
Somnath (m), Lord Shiva
Sona (f), gold
Sonal (f), golden
Sonali (f), golden
Sonakshi (f), golden-eyed
Sonika (f), golden
Soorat (f), beauty
Sopan (m), steps
Soumil (m), a friend
Soumitra (m), Lakshman, brother of Lord Rama
Soumya (f), handsome
Soumyakanti (m), handsome
Sourabh (m), fragrance
Sourabhi (f), fragrance; the celestial cow
Souren(dra) (m), of the sun
Sourish (m), Lord Vishnu
Sristi (f), creation
Srijan (m), creation
Stavita (f), praised
Stuti (f), praise

Sual (m), asked for
Subal (m), a friend of Lord Krishna
Subarna (f), of the colour of gold
Subash (m), fragrance
Subbarao (m), auspicious
Subhadra (m), source of great welfare
Subhadra (f), sister of Lord Krishna, wife of Arjuna
Subhagya (f), lucky
Subhan (m), aware
Subhash (m), well-spoken
Subhashini (f), well-spoken
Subinay (m), humble
Subrata (m), devoted to what is right
Subrata (f), devoted to husband
Suchandra (f), beautiful
Sucharita (f), of good character
Sucheta (f), with a beautiful mind
Suchi (f), radiant
Suchira (f), tasteful
Suchita (f), beautiful
Suchitra (f), beautiful picture
Sudakshina (f), wife of King Dilip
Sudama (m), Lord Krishna's friend
Sudarshan (m), handsome

Sudarshana (f), handsome
Sudeep (m), bright
Sudeepa (f), bright
Sudeepta (f), bright
Sudesh (m), country
Sudeshna (f), wife of King Virata
Sudha (f), nectar
Sudhakar (m), the moon
Sudhamay (m), full of nectar
Sudhamayi (f), full of nectar
Sudhanshu (m), the moon
Sudhi (m), scholar
Sudhindra (m) lord of knowledge
Sudhir (m), great scholar; calm
Sudhira (f), calm
Sudipta (f), bright
Sudipti (f), brightness
Sugata (m), a name of the Buddha
Sugita (f), beautifully sung
Sugouri (f), Goddess Parvati
Sugreev (m), man with a beautiful neck
Suhag (f), love
Suhail (m), moon-glow
Suhaila (f), moon-glow
Suhas (m), smiling beautifully
Suhasini (f), ever-smiling

Suhina (f), beautiful
Suhrid (m), well-disposed
Suhrit (m), well-disposed
Suhrita (f), well-disposed
Sujala (f), affectionate
Sujan (m), honest
Sujata (f), well-bred
Sujay (m), victory
Sujaya (f), victory
Sujash (m), illustrious
Sujit (m), winner
Sukanta (m), handsome
Sukanya (f), comely woman
Sukesh (m), with beautiful hair
Sukeshi (f), with beautiful hair
Suketu (m), a Yaksha king
Sukhamay (m), pleasurable
Sukhdev (m), giver of bliss
Sukrit (m), pious
Sukriti (f), good deed
Sukumar (m), soft; meritorious
Sukumari (f), soft; meritorious
Sulabha (f), easy; natural
Sulakshana (f), well-brought up
Sulalita (f), very pleasing
Sulekh (m), beautifully written
Sulekha (f), beautiful writing
Suloch (f), one with beautiful eyes
Sulochan (m), one with beautiful eyes
Sulochana (f), one with beautiful eyes
Sultan (m), king
Sultana (f), queen
Suman (m), flower
Sumana (f), noble
Sumanolata (f), flowery creeper
Sumant (m), wise
Sumanta (m), wise
Sumantra (m), friend of King Dasarath
Sumati (f), wisdom
Sumedh (m), clever
Sumedha (f), wise
Sumeet, Sumit (m), a good friend
Sumita (f), a good friend
Sumitra (f), name of the mother of Lakshmana
Sumitra (m), good friend
Sunanda (m), very pleasing
Sunanda (f), Uma, wife of Lord Shiva
Sunandini (f), happy
Sunandita (f), happy
Sunasi (m), Lord Indra
Sunayana (f), a woman with lovely eyes
Sunayani (f), a woman with lovely eyes
Sundar (m), handsome

- **Sundari** (f), beautiful
- **Sundha** (f), a character in Ramayana
- **Suneet** (m), of good principles; prudent
- **Suneeti** (f), mother of Dhruva
- **Sunetra** (f), one with beautiful eyes
- **Sunil** (m), blue; sapphire
- **Sunila** (f), blue
- **Sunirmal** (m), pure
- **Suniti** (f), good principles
- **Suparna** (m), Lord Vishnu
- **Suparna** (f), leafy
- **Suprabha** (f), radiant
- **Suprakash** (m), manifested
- **Supratik** (m), cupid
- **Supratim** (m), beautiful image
- **Supriti** (f), true love
- **Supriya** (m), beloved
- **Supriya** (f), beloved
- **Supti** (f), sleep
- **Sur** (m), a musical note
- **Suraiya** (f), beautiful
- **Suraj** (m), the sun
- **Surajit** (m), god
- **Suraksha** (f), protection
- **Surama** (f), very pleasing
- **Surekha** (f), beautifully drawn
- **Suranjan** (m), pleasing
- **Suranjana** (f), pleasing
- **Suren** (m), Lord Indra
- **Suresh** (m), Lord Indra
- **Surina** (f), a goddess
- **Suruchi** (f), good taste
- **Surya** (m), the sun
- **Suryabhan** (m), the sun
- **Suryakanta** (m), a jewel
- **Suryashankar** (m), Lord Shiva
- **Sushanta** (m), quiet
- **Sushanti** (f), peace
- **Sushil** (m), well-behaved
- **Sushila** (f), well-behaved
- **Sushama** (f), beauty
- **Sushobhan** (m), very beautiful
- **Sushobhana** (f) very beautiful
- **Sushrut** (m), well-heard
- **Sushruta** (m), son of sage Viswamitra
- **Susita** (f), white
- **Susmita** (f), smiling
- **Sutanuka** (f), beautiful
- **Sutapa** (f), seeker of God
- **Sutej** (m), lustre
- **Suvan** (m), the sun
- **Suvarna** (f), golden
- **Suvimal** (m), pure
- **Suvarnmala** (f), golden necklace
- **Suvarnaprabha** (f), lustre of gold
- **Suvarnarekha** (f), ray of gold
- **Suyash** (m), illustrious

Swagata (f), welcome
Swaha (f), wife of Agni, the lord of fire
Swami (m), master
Swaminath (m), the Lord Almighty
Swapan (m), dream
Swapna (f), dreamlike
Swapnali (f), dream
Swapnasundari (f), woman of dreams
Swapnil (m), dreamlike

Swarnalata (f), lustrous
Swarup (m), truth
Swarupa (f), true
Swasti (f), welfare
Swati (f), name of a star
Swayambhu (m), Lord Shiva
Swetaketu (m), an ancient sage
Syamantak (m), a jewel of Lord Vishnu

T

Tabassum (f), a flower
Tahir (m), holy
Taizeen (m), encouragement
Taj (m), crown
Tajdar (m), crowned
Talat (m), prayer
Talib (m), divine
Talleen (m), absorbed
Tamal (m), a tree with very dark bark
Tamali (f), a tree with very dark bark
Tamalika (f), belonging to a place full of Tamal
Tamanna (f), desire
Tamasa (f), a river; darkness
Tamasi (f), night
Tambura (f), a musical instrument
Tamkinat (m), pomp
Tamonash (m), destroyer of ignorance
Tanay (m), son
Tanaya (f), daughter
Tanika (f), rope
Tanima (f), slenderness
Tanmay (m), absorbed
Tanmaya (f), absorbed
Tannishtha (f), dedicated
Tanu (f), body
Tanuj (m), son
Tanuja (f), daughter
Tanuka (f), slender
Tanushri (f), beautiful
Tanveer (m), enlightened
Tapan (m), the sun
Tapani (f), the river Godavari
Tapas (m), ascetic
Tapasendra (m), Lord Shiva
Tapasi (f), a female ascetic
Tapasranjan (m), Lord Vishnu
Tapati (f), the sun's daughter
Tapomay (m), full of moral virtue
Tapti (f), a river
Tara (f), star; wife of Lord Brihaspati
Tarak (m), protector
Taraka (f), star
Tarakini (f), starry night
Tarachand (m), star
Tarakeshwar (m), Lord Shiva
Tarakeshwari (f), Goddess Parvati
Taraknath (m), Lord Shiva
Taral (m), restless
Tarala (f), honeybee
Tarana (f), a musical composition

Taranga (m), wave
Tarangini (f), river
Tarani (f), boat
Tarannum (f), melody
Taraprashad (m), star
Tarik (m), one who crosses the river of life
Tarika (f), starlet
Tarini (f), Goddess Parvati
Tariq (m), morning star
Tarit (m), lightning
Taritprabha (f), lightning
Taru (f), tree
Tarulata (f), creeper
Tarun (m), young
Taruni (f), young girl
Tarunika (f), young girl
Tarunima (f), youth
Taruntapan (m), morning sun
Tasneem (f), salute of paradise
Tatini (f), river
Tathagata (m), the Buddha
Tausiq (m), reinforcement
Teertha (f), place of pilgrimage
Teerthankar (m), a Jain saint
Teesta (f), a river
Tehzeeb (f), elegance
Tejal (f), lustrous
Tejas (m), lustre; brilliance
Tejaswini (f), lustrous

Tejaswi (f), lustrous
Tejeshwar (m), the sun
Tejomay (m), glorious
Thakur (m), leader; God
Thumri (f), light classical melody
Tilak (m), auspicious spot on the forehead
Tilaka (f), a kind of necklace
Tilottama (f), a celestial maiden
Timila (f), a musical instrument
Timir (m), darkness
Timirbaran (m), dark
Tirtha (m), holy place
Titiksha (f), forgiveness
Titir (m), a bird
Toral (f), a folk heroine
Toshan (m), satisfaction
Trailokva (m), the three worlds
Trambak (m), Lord Shiva
Tribhuvan (m), the three worlds
Tridhara (f), the river Ganga
Tridib (m), heaven
Trigun (m), the three dimensions
Triguna (f), maya or illusion; Goddess Durga
Triguni (f), the three dimensions

Trikaya (f), three dimensional
Trilochan (m), Lord Shiva
Trilochana (f), Goddess Durga
Trilok (m), the three worlds
Trilokesh (m), Lord Shiva
Trinayani (f), Goddess Durga
Trinetra (f), Goddess Durga
Triparna (f), leaf of sacred Bael
Tripta (f), satisfied
Tripti (f), satisfaction
Tripurari (m), Lord Shiva
Tripurasundari (f), Goddess Parvati
Tripuri (f), Goddess Parvati
Trisha (f), thirst
Trishala (f), mother of Lord Mahavir
Trishanku (m), a king of the Surya dynasty
Trishna (f), thirst
Triveni (f), confluence of three sacred rivers
Trivikram (m), Lord Vishnu
Triyama (f), night
Tufan (m), storm
Tuhin (m), snow
Tuhinsurra (m), white as snow
Tuhina (f), snow
Tukaram (m), a poet saint
Tulika (f), brush
Tulasi (f), the sacred basil
Tulsidas (m), a famous saint
Tushar (m), snow
Tusharkana (f), a particle of snow
Tusharkanti (m), Lord Shiva
Tusharsuvra (m), white as snow
Tyagraja (m), a famous poet

U

Udar (m), generous
Uday (m), appearance
Udayan (m), rising; name of king of Avanti
Udayachal (m), eastern horizon
Uddhar (m), liberation
Uddhav (m), Lord Krishna's friend
Udit (m), risen
Udita (f), one who has risen
Uditi (f), rising
Udyam (m), effort
Udyan (m), garden
Ujagar (m), bright
Ujala (m), bright
Ujas (f), bright
Ujjaini (f), an ancient city
Ujwal, Ujjala (m), bright
Ujwala, Ujjala (f), bright
Ulhas (m), happiness
Ulka (f), meteor
Ulupi (f), wife of Arjuna, the Pandava prince
Uma (f), Goddess Parvati
Umanant, Umakant (m), Lord Shiva
Umanand (m), Lord Shiva
Umaprasad (m), blessing of Goddess Parvati
Umashankar (m), Lord Shiva

Umed (m), hope
Umesh (m), Lord Shiva
Umika (f), Goddess Parvati
Umrao (m & f), noble
Unmesh (m), revelation
Unnat (m), energized
Unnati (f), progress
Upala (f), sandy shore
Upagupta (m), name of a Buddhist monk
Upama (f), simile
Upamanyu (m), name of a devoted pupil
Upasana (f), veneration
Upendra (m), Lord Vishnu
Ura (f), the heart
Urja (f), energy
Urjita (m), energized
Urmi (f), wave
Urmimala (f), garland of waves
Urmila, Urmil (f), the wife of Lakshmana (brother of Lord Rama)
Urna (f), cover
Urshila (f), outstanding
Urshita (f), firm
Urvashi (f), a celestial maiden
Urvi (f), the earth
Usha (f), dawn
Ushakanta (m), the sun
Ushakiran (f), the first rays

Ushashi (f), morning
Usri (f), a river
Utanka (m), a disciple of the sage Veda
Utkarsha (m), advancement
Utpal (m), lotus
Utpala (f), lotus

Utsa (f), spring
Uttam (m), best
Uttar (m), son of king Virata
Uttara (f), daughter of king Virata
Uttiya (m), a name in Buddhist literature
Utsav (m), celebration

V

Vachan (m), speech
Vagdevi (f), Goddess Saraswati
Vahini (f), flowing
Vaibhav (m), riches
Vaidehi (f), name of Sita
Vaijayanti (f), a garland of Lord Vishnu
Vaijayantimala (f), a garland of Lord Vishnu
Vaijnath (m), Lord Shiva
Vaishali (f), an ancient city of India
Vaishavi, Vaishnodevi (f), Goddess Parvati
Vajra (m), Lord Krishna's greatgrandson; diamond
Vajradhar (m), Lord Indra
Vajrapani (m), Lord Indra
Vallabh (m), beloved
Vallari (f), Goddess Parvati; creeper
Valli (f), creeper
Valmiki, Valmik (m), the author of the epic Ramayana
Vama (f), woman
Vaman (m), fifth incarnation of Lord Vishnu
Vanaja (f), a forest girl
Vanajit (m), lord of the forest
Vanamala (f), garland of forests
Vanani (f), forest
Vandana (f), worship
Vanhi (f), fire
Vanhishikha (f), flame
Vani (f), muse, Goddess Saraswati
Vanita (f), woman
Varada (f), Goddess Lakshmi
Varana (f), a river
Vardhaman (m), Lord Mahavir
Vari (f), water; sea
Varij (m), lotus
Varindra (m), lord of the ocean
Varsha (f), rain
Varisha (f), rain
Varun (m), lord of the sea
Varuna (f), wife of the lord of the sea; name of a river
Varuni (f), wife of the lord of the sea; Goddess Durga
Vasant (m), spring
Vasanti (f), of spring
Vasavi (f), wife of Indra
Vasistha (m), name of a sage
Vasudev (m), father of Lord Krishna

Vasudha (f), the earth
Vasumati (f), the earth
Vasundhara (f), the earth
Vatsal (m), affectionate
Vatsala (f), affectionate
Ved (m), a sacred text
Vedmohan (m), Lord Krishna
Vedanga (m), meaning of Vedas
Vedi (f), altar
Vedika (f), altar; a river in India
Vedprakash (m), light of the Vedas
Vedvalli (f), joy of the Vedas
Vedavrata (m), vow of the Vedas
Veena (f), lute
Veenapani (f), Goddess Saraswati
Veera (f), brave
Vela (f), time
Veni (m), Lord Krishna
Venimadhav (m), Lord Krishna
Vetravati (f), a river in India
Vibha (f), night
Vibhas (m), decoration; light
Vibhat (m), dawn
Vibhavari (f), starry night
Vibhishan (m), a character from the epic Ramayana
Vibhu (m), all-pervading
Vibhuti (f), great personality
Vidula (f), the moon
Vidur (m), a friend of Lord Krishna
Vidya (f), learning
Vidyadhar (m), learned
Vidyasagar (m), ocean of learning
Vidyul (f), lightning
Vidyut (m & f), lightning
Vighnesh (m), Lord Ganesh
Vihanga (m), bird
Vijay (m), victor
Vijaya (f), victory of Goddess Durga
Vijeta (f), victorious
Vijendra, Vijayendra (m), victorious
Vijul (f), a silk-cotton tree
Vikas (m), development
Vikesh (m), the moon
Vikram (m), bravery
Vikramaditya (m), a famous king
Vikramájit (m), a famous king
Vikranta (m), brave
Vilas (m), play
Vilasini (f), playful
Vilina (f), dedicated
Vilok (m), to see
Vilokan (m), gaze

Vimal (m), pure
Vimala, Vimla (f), pure
Vinay (m), modesty
Vinaya (f), modest
Vinayak (m), Lord Ganesh
Vindhya (f), knowledge
Vineet (m), unassuming
Vineeta (f), unassuming
Vinesh (m), godly
Vinod (m), pleasing
Vinodini (f), pleasing
Vipasa (f), a river
Vipin (m), forest
Viplab (m), floating; revolution
Vipra (m), a priest
Vipul (m), plenty
Vipula (f), plenty
Vir (m), brave
Viraj (f), splendour
Viral (m), priceless
Virendra (m), brave lord
Viresh (m), brave lord
Virata (f), bravery
Vishakha (f), a star
Vishal (m), immense
Vishala (f), wide; spacious
Vishalakshi (f), large-eyed
Vishwambhar (m), the lord
Vishaya (f), subject
Vishweshwar (m), the lord
Vishesh (m), special
Vishnu (m), Lord Vishnu
Vishnupriya (f), Goddess Lakshmi
Vishram (m), rest
Vishwamitra (m), a sage
Vishwanath (m), the lord
Vishwesh (m), the Lord Almighty
Vismay (m), surprise
Viswas (m), trust
Vithala, Vitthal (m), Lord Vishnu
Vivek (m), right judgement; conscience
Viveka (f), right judgement; conscience
Vivekananda (m), joy of discrimination
Vrajakishore (m), Lord Krishna
Vrajabala (f), girl from Mathura and its neighbourhood
Vrajesh (m), Lord Krishna
Vrajamohan (m), Lord Krishna
Vrajanandan (m), Lord Krishna
Vrinda (f), basil; Radha
Vrishin (m), peacock
Vritti (f), nature; temperament
Vyanjana (f), rhetorical suggestion
Vyasa (m), the author of Mahabharata

See also entries under *B*

W

Wahab (m), large-hearted
Waheeda (f), beautiful
Wajidali (m), obsessed; involved

Wali (m), protector
Wamika (f), Goddess Durga
Wamil (f), beautiful

Y

Yadav (m), Lord Krishna's clan
Yadunandan (m), Lord Krishna
Yadunath (m), Lord Krishna
Yaduraj (m), Lord Krishna
Yagnya (f), sacred fire
Yajas (m), worship
Yajati (m), a king of the Chandra dynasty
Yamini (f), night
Yamuna (f), a holy river
Yashas (m), success
Yashila (f), successful
Yashna (f), prayer
Yashovanta, Yasvant (m), famous
Yashoda, Jasoda (f), mother of Lord Krishna; giver of success
Yashodhara (f), mother of Lord Buddha
Yashomati (f), successful
Yashpal (m), protector of fame
Yasksini (f), celestial being
Yasmin (f), a flower; Chameli
Yatin (m), an ascetic
Yatindra (m), a great sage
Yog, Jog (m), united; deep meditation; Yoga
Yogamaya (f), the magical power of Yoga
Yogas (m), deep meditation
Yogendra (m), master of Yoga
Yogin (m), ascetic
Yogini (f), a devotee; meditator
Yogesh (m), Lord Krishna
Yogeshwar (m), Lord Krishna
Yosha (f), woman
Yoshita (f), woman
Yugal (m), pair
Yugalkishore (m), a name of Lord Krishna
Yuri (m), lily
Yusuf (m), God's chosen
Yuvati (f), young girl
Yuvaraj (m), prince

See also entries under *J*

Z

Zachariah (m), God's remembrance
Zafar (m), achievement
Zain (m), good light
Zahid (m), intelligent; pious
Zahira (f), expression
Zaki (m), saintly
Zareen (f), golden

Zarina (f), queen
Zeenat (f), glory
Zenia (f), a flower
Zia (m & f), enlightened
Zila (f), shade
Zohra (f), the planet Jupiter
Zuber, Zubair (m), pure
Zulekha (f), beautiful

SOME MORE NAMES

A

Aruna (f), dawn
Aruni (f), dawn
Ayog (m), institution
Ayushmati (f), one who has a long life

B

Bahula (f), abundant; born under the Pleiades
Bandhula (m/f), charming
Bhavini (f), beautiful; illustrious

D

Dhara (f), current of water

H

Hemambar (m), golden sky or golden dress

J

Jheel (f), lake

K

Kaustav (m), a legendary gem; a gem worn by Lord Vishnu
Keshi (f), a woman with beautiful hair
Kurangi (f), deer

M

Maitripal (m), protector of friendship
Mudita (f), unopened

N

Nalin (m), lotus
Nauka (f), boat

P

Panini (m), the great scholar-grammarian
Parakram (m), strength
Pavani (f), purifier; Ganga
Phenil (m), foamy
Pranjal (m), straight
Prasham (m), tranquillity
Pravar (m), most excellent

R

Ranjini (f), pleasing
Rashmil (m), silken
Ratnanabha (m), Lord Vishnu

Rijuta (f), straightness
Ripudaman (m), one who has defeated enemies or passions

S

Sadhvi (f), chaste woman
Sarvadaman (m), one who subdues everybody
Sharika (f), Goddess Durga
Shinjini (f), anklebells
Shreela (f), lustrous
Shyamangi, (f), dark-complexioned
Soham (m), I am He (God)
Surdeep (m), lamp of music
Suryakanti (f), sun's rays

T

Tarjani (f), the first finger
Trinetra (f), Goddess Parvati

V

Vaishnavi (f), Goddess Durga; Ganga
Vanadurga (f), Goddess Parvati
Vishnumaya (f), Goddess Parvati